THE

FIRST BOOK OF KNOWLEDGE

THE FIRST BOOK OF KNOWLEDGE

FREDERICK GUTHRIE

GYAN

Published by

Gyan Publishing House
5, Ansari Road
Daryaganj, New Delhi-110002
Phone: 011-47034999, 9811692060
E-mail: books@gyanbooks.com

Distribution Network
gyanbooks.com
India, USA, Canada, UK, Australia

ISBN: 978-93-7169-236-6 (PB)

First Published, 1881

2nd Impression 2025

Printed at: Gyan Press, Delhi.

THE FIRST BOOK OF KNOWLEDGE
Author: FREDERICK GUTHRIE

THE

FIRST BOOK OF KNOWLEDGE.

BY

FREDERICK GUTHRIE, F.R.S.,

Professor of Physics at the Normal School of Science, South Kensington.

London:

MARCUS WARD & CO., 67, 68, CHANDOS STREET,

And ROYAL ULSTER WORKS, BELFAST.

1881.

INTRODUCTORY.

WHAT THIS BOOK IS ABOUT, AND HOW TO USE IT.

Clay is a stuff. A brick is a thing. I want boys and girls, and so, by-and-by, everybody, to know something about stuffs and things. Therefore, in this First Book of Knowledge I have striven to make clear what stuffs are, and how things are made from them. So I take such a house as most of us live in, and show, first, of what stuffs, and how, its parts are made, and I speak as near to the beginning as I can of those things which are first used as the house is being built. But as I find that bricks and mortar are made by the help of coal, I begin with a few words about coal; then I speak of what may be called the trimmings of the house—such as paint and paper; then of pots, and pans, and such; then of lighting and heating, then of clothing, then of food, then of cleaning, then of writing and printing.

When this book is used by a teacher, he should get as many as he can of the stuffs and things spoken of—such as a lump of clay, a brick, a bit of lime, a bit of iron ore, a bit of iron, and so on. Lists of such things are given as they are wanted. Each Part of the Book is broken into lesser parts marked by numbers, such as IX. Each lesser part forms about one Lesson. The Questions given at the end of each lesson are only samples. As the teacher gets further on, he will of course ask questions about what has gone before. In teaching, he should only use this book as a guide, and he should be able to give other and more knowledge than is given here.

No one man or woman can fully understand all these things; so I have asked some of my friends to help me in those parts which they best know, and I have got some children to help me in the same way. My thanks are chiefly due to the following:—Dr. J. H. Gladstone, F.R.S.; Mr. T. Healey, Professor Judd, F.R.S.; Professor Roberts, F.R.S.; the Misses J. and L. Sharpe, and Mr. J. Harris Stone, M.A.

I shall be glad to hear from anyone who has anything to say about the book as to how it might be bettered; and, although I may not be able to answer them, I shall take care that what they may say shall be well weighed for use in other editions.

FREDERICK GUTHRIE.

South Kensington, 1881.

CONTENTS.

PART I.

THINGS AND STUFFS USED FOR HOUSE BUILDING.

(For Wood, see Part III., page 42.)

PART II.

WHAT MATTER IS MADE OF.

ELEMENTS. AIR. FIRE. FLAME. WATER.

PART III.

WOOD.

PART IV.

HEATING AND LIGHTING.

PART V.

FINISHING AND FURNISHING.

PART VI.

CLOTHING.

PART VII.

FOOD.

PART VIII.

CLEANING.

PART IX.

WRITING AND PRINTING.

PART I.

THINGS AND STUFFS USED FOR HOUSE-BUILDING.

I.

Coal, Ashes, Cinders, Coke, Breeze.

THINGS TO BE SEEN.—*A piece of coal—a piece of limestone—a piece of coal with some plant remains in it—a piece of limestone with some shells in it—ashes, cinders, coke, and breeze.*

§ 1. **Coal.**—When wood or woody matter—such as roots, bark, leaves, moss, peat, and so on—lies buried in the earth for a very long time, it changes into coal. Wherever coal is now found, there were once forests, or woods, or peat, or else mouths of rivers, or other places where plants grew, or their dead parts, leaves and branches and roots, got heaped together. Then such places got covered with water, often because they sank below the level of the sea, and the sea covered them, and they were at the bottom of the sea. Then the mud which rivers bring down to the sea sank down and covered them, and the shells and skeletons of dead sea animals fell also upon them, so that they got covered deeper and deeper. When such places rose again above the sea-level, the sea rolled off them, and the rain washed the sea-salt off them, so that when the wind blew seeds upon them, the seeds struck root, and plants again grew. This sinking and rising of the earth has sometimes happened many times in the same place. So that on digging down we often come upon several layers of coal, called seams of coal; and between the separate seams is the earth which once formed the bottom of the sea, and which has got hardened into rocks. Sometimes a part of the land on which plants grew has sunk down and formed a hollow or basin so far from the sea that the sea has not rolled in upon it. Such hollows have then got filled with water from rivers and rain, and have become lakes. Then, as before, mud has settled upon the bottom, along with the shells and skeletons of fresh-water animals; and so this may go on again and again. So the plants have got buried, and, after thousands and thousands of years, have become coal. Of course, therefore, when one seam of coal lies above another, the upper one has been formed last, and pieces of such newer coal often have the shapes which they had when they were buried, such as tree-trunks and seed. But such plants are often unlike those now growing above them; and this shows either that the climates of countries have changed very much, or that the plants themselves have gradually altered through one plant not being quite like the plant from whose seed it sprang.

§ 2. **Ashes, Cinders, Coke, Breeze.**—When coal is thoroughly burnt in an open fireplace, nothing is left but ashes, which are nearly white, and very soft and light. When coal is not thoroughly burnt, it is cinder. The stuff which falls through the bars is partly ash and partly cinder. If this mixture is put on a sieve and sifted, the ashes fall through and leave the cinders. When coal is baked in an iron box which has a hole in it, a lot of gas (see § 40) and tar comes out of the hole; and when the box has got cold and is opened, a hard, gritty, black mass is found, which is called COKE. When broken into small pieces, coke is called BREEZE. Both coke and breeze can be burnt in an open fireplace, and they leave behind just the same ash that coal does.

Questions.—What has coal been made of? How has it been made? How does it come that coal is found in "seams"—that is, layers—between which there are layers of rock? Why are shells often found in such layers of rock? How is it that the remains of plants found in coal belong to plants unlike those now growing on the ground above the coal? What is left when coal is thoroughly burnt? What is left when it is only partly burnt? How is coke made? What is breeze?

II.

Concrete, Mortar.

THINGS TO BE SEEN.—*Flint—sand—pebbles—limestone—quick-lime—slaked lime—chalk—marble—the slaking of lime—the mixing of mortar.*

§ 3. **Concrete.**—In order to get a firm place for a house to stand on, the mould and earth are dug away where the walls are to be, and into the ditches or trenches so formed some concrete is put. This concrete is made of sand, pebbles, lime, and water. The sand used is found upon the sea-shore and in river-beds, or forming layers (sometimes hundreds of feet thick) in the earth. It has been formed by the breaking of flints or the crumbling to pieces of granite and some other rocks. Sand and gravel and many pebbles are often little else than grains or lumps of silica, which is a body containing two elements (see § 29). Pebbles used for concrete differ from grains of sand only in their larger size. The lime has to be made; and it can be made either out of chalk, or marble, or other kind of limestone. These three things are little else but lime united with a gas called carbonic acid (see §§ 8, 30, 31, 32). Whole mountains are made of such kinds of limestone. The way lime is made out of limestone is as follows:—A hollow tower of stone or bricks, called a lime-kiln, is built, having a small hole at the bottom, and being open at the top. A coal-fire is lighted at the bottom, and lumps of limestone and coal are thrown in from the top.

The coal burns away, and the heat which it gives drives the gas (carbonic acid) out of the limestone, and leaves lumps of lime called quick-lime. When about its own weight of water is poured upon quick-lime, the lime swells up, gets very hot, and falls to pieces as a white powder called slaked lime. To make the concrete, eight parts by weight of pebbles, four of sand, and one of quick-lime are mixed together with water so as to form a thick pasty mass. When this is put into the trenches, it gets after a time as hard as stone, and makes a firm, smooth, dry place for the bricks of the wall to rest on.

§ 4. **Mortar.**—Mortar is made in the same way as concrete, only no pebbles are used. The best sand to use is river-sand; and if sea-sand is used, it should be washed in fresh water to get rid of the sea-salt which is in it.

Questions.—What is concrete made of? Where is sand found? What has sand been made from? What are pebbles? What is limestone? How is quick-lime made? How is slaked lime made from quick-lime? What happens when water is poured on quick-lime? How is mortar made?

III.

Bricks, Clay, Tiles, Chimney-pots, Drain-pipes.

THINGS TO BE SEEN.—*Some dry and wet clay—a brick—pieces of earthenware.*

§ 5. **Bricks.**—Bricks are made of CLAY. Pure clay is white; but the clay of which common bricks are made is brown, yellow, grey, or red, and sometimes bluish or nearly black. These colours are usually caused by iron rust. When rocks are exposed to the weather—that is, to air, and rain, and frost (see § 33), and sunshine—they gradually crumble to pieces, and are carried down by brooks into rivers, and by rivers into lakes or the sea. Some parts of the rocks are, indeed, quite dissolved, just as salt is dissolved by water (see § 116). Others are ground by being rubbed together in the rivers to the fineness of grains of mud, others to sand, others to gravel or pebbles. When the river enters the lake or the sea, the largest pieces of solid settle down soonest, and so rest near the river's mouth, while the finest settle last, and so are carried furthest. The clay which forms part of many rocks is broken into very fine particles indeed, and so it is carried out a long way, and is separated from the gravel and sand. Clay is thus formed at the bottoms of lakes and seas. And wherever clay is found, that place must at one time, ages and ages ago, have been at the bottom of water, although now it may be far above the sea-level. Some clay is moist; some is so dry and hard, that it has to be ground with water before it can be used for brick-making. To make bricks, the clay which has been dug up is broken and exposed to the air and frost through the winter months. It is then worked or kneaded with enough water to make it very stiff, and all pebbles are carefully picked out. Then the brick-maker takes a mould, which is a wooden or iron box of the shape of the brick, having neither top nor bottom. He strews some sand on a board, and having wetted the inside of the mould, strews some sand on it also. This prevents the clay sticking to the mould. He then puts the mould upon the board, and fills it with clay higher than the edge of the mould. The top is then smoothed off by a stick, and the mould and brick taken away to a flat floor. The raw brick is taken out of the mould and placed flat on the floor, where it rests till it gets dry enough to bear handling without injury. The raw bricks, when thus partly dry, are trimmed with a knife, and piled on one another in low walls, in such a way that there are spaces between them for the air to go round. The tops of such walls are sometimes covered with straw, or otherwise roofed, to keep off the rain. After being thus further dried, the raw bricks are ready for burning. There are two ways of burning bricks: they are burnt either in KILNS or CLAMPS. A Kiln is a brick house nearly square, and about as high as it is wide. Inside are arched brick floors, with holes in them, and the raw bricks being put upon these floors, some fuel which blazes is put in at a hole at the bottom of one of the walls, so that the flame playing amongst the bricks bakes them. The Clamp, which is more often used, and is often called a kiln, is built of the raw bricks themselves. A layer of these being laid on the earth, a mixture of small coal, breeze, and cinders is strewn upon them, then another layer of bricks a little way apart, then more fuel, and so on. In building the clamp, hollow spaces are left, which serve as chimneys; and by closing the outer ends of one or other of these, the draught can be regulated. This regulation of the draught is also done by plastering wet clay at various places on the outside, so as to stop the draught there; for where there is no air the fire is smothered. When the fuel is burnt out and the clamp is cool, the bricks are taken out, and are now found to be full of small holes, hard, and not to be softened by water. They are also found to have shrunk in size. The holes in the bricks let the soft mortar enter them a little way, so that when the mortar sets, or hardens, the bricks are not only stuck but clamped together.

§ 6. **Tiles, Chimney-pots, and Drain-pipes.**—These are also made of clay. The clay must be purer than that which may be used for common bricks, and the stones more carefully taken out. Sand is often mixed with the clay. To make glazed tiles or drain-pipes, which have to be waterproof, common salt is heated in the kiln along with the tiles or drain-pipes. CROCKERY of all kinds is also made with clay (see § 84).

§ 7. **Slate.**—When clay has been in a dry state for a very long time, and has been pressed very much by other rocks, it can no longer be softened by water, and it can, when taken freshly from the quarry, be split in flakes or sheets by a chisel. It is called SLATE. Some time after being taken from the quarry, especially if the slate is acted on by frosts and thaws, it can no longer be split. Slate is used in buildings for covering roofs, for cisterns, and sometimes for mantelpieces.

Questions.—What is meant by the weather? What happens to rocks when they are acted on by the weather? How has clay been made? In brick-making, what is done to the clay to make it fit for bricks? How are bricks made of the right shape? How is the clay stopped from sticking to the mould? How are bricks dried? What is a brick kiln? What is a brick clamp? What kind of fuel is used in a kiln? What fuel is used in a clamp? How is the heating in a clamp regulated? How does a baked brick differ from a dry one? What is the use of the holes in the brick? How does clay used for tiles, chimney-pots, and drain-pipes differ from brick clay? How are such things glazed? What is slate? What is it used for?

IV.

Limestone, Marble, Sandstone, Granite, Plaster, Thatch, Shingles.

THINGS TO BE SEEN.—*Pieces of limestone—marble—sandstone—granite—dry plaster of Paris—the setting of plaster of Paris when mixed with water.*

§ 8. **Limestone.**—Some very small animals which live in the sea take the carbonate of lime from the sea, and use it to make their shells or skeletons. When such animals die, the carbonate of lime which they had gathered settles to the bottom of the sea, and makes in time beds, which may be hundreds of feet thick. This slowly hardens, and is then called limestone. If this sea-bottom rises above the general level of the sea, the sea drains away from it, and the limestone is then, of course, found inland, away from the sea, just as coal is so found (see § 1).

§ 9. **Marble.**—When limestone is acted on by water, and more of the same gas as it already has (carbonic acid), it becomes hard enough to be polished. It is then called marble.

§ 10. **Sandstone.**—When beds of sand become wetted

through with water containing silica (see § 3), a hardening takes place, much like the hardening of mortar, and the loose sand is changed into sandstone.

§ 11. **Granite.**—Granite is a rock which seems to have once been melted, and to have cooled slowly far underground, and while it was much squeezed. Granite is a mixture of several different things. There are little black or white glittering scales in it, called mica. Then there are transparent crystals—that is, crystals easily seen through—called quartz, and larger milky-white or pink crystals, called felspar. In some kinds of granite one can see crystals of felspar an inch or two long.

§ 12. **Plaster or Gypsum.**—Plaster is found in the earth as a rock. A fifth of its weight is water. When the gypsum is heated in a kiln, not too strongly, it gives off this water, and becomes so soft that it can easily be crumbled and ground to a fine powder. When so dried and ground, it is called plaster of Paris. When this plaster of Paris is mixed with even so much water as to make a very thin cream, it becomes hot and dry, just as quick-lime does. It becomes hard, and because its surface when dry is smooth, it is used for taking casts. The mouldings on the cornices of rooms and the ornaments of ceilings are casts made of plaster of Paris. The ceilings of rooms are made of plaster, or plaster and mortar, with which are mixed the hairs of cows and oxen, which hairs are scraped from the hides when hides are tanned. The hair makes the plaster less crumbly; it binds the brittle plaster together (see § 97).

§ 13. **Thatch.**—The roofs of houses are often made of straw or of rushes. Straw does not last very long, but a roof of rushes may last twenty or thirty years. The rush is laid on thickly, and bound to the open woodwork of the roof; then more is bound to that, and so on. Thatched roofs, like houses built entirely of wood, are dangerous to neighbouring houses if they catch fire, and they themselves are in great danger from neighbouring fires. So wooden houses and thatched houses are not allowed to be built in towns; but in the country, where straw or rushes are plentiful, or slate scarce, thatched roofs are made, and, being thick, they keep the heat in in winter, and the heat out in summer.

§ 14. **Shingles.**—Sometimes (but in this country not often) the roofs of houses are made of little boards the size and shape of tiles. These are nailed to the frame of the roof in such a way that they overlap one another. Such wooden tiles are called shingles.

Questions.—What is limestone made of? What is it made by? What is it made from? How is it that limestone is found far from the sea? What is marble? How has sandstone been made? How has granite been made? What is it made of? Where is gypsum found? What is the difference between gypsum and plaster of Paris? How is plaster of Paris made from gypsum? What happens when plaster of Paris is mixed with water? What is plaster of Paris used for? Why is hair mixed with plaster? What is thatch made of? Why is it not used in towns? What is the good of thatch? What is the harm of it? What are shingles?

V.

Metals in General, Iron, Slag.

THINGS TO BE SEEN.—*Pieces of iron ore—limestone—coke—slag—cast-iron—wrought-iron.*

§ 15. **Metals in General.**—There are four metals chiefly used in building a house—IRON, LEAD, COPPER, and ZINC. Iron is used where great strength is wanted; it is cheap. Lead is used where its softness is of advantage, as when one wants to cover wood from the rain. The lead can be easily bent into any shape; it does not rust away, like iron. Zinc is dearer than either lead or iron. It is harder than lead, but softer than iron; and it has this advantage over lead, that its rust is not very poisonous, while the rust of lead is very poisonous. Zinc does not rust away, like iron, though it tarnishes on the surface, even in the purest damp air. In places where coal is burnt, the zinc is eaten away because the air of such places is acid. Copper is dear, and its rust is poisonous, but is easily cleaned. Of these four metals, copper is the only one which is even sometimes found in nature in the pure state—that is, as a metal. All the three others, and copper generally, have to be got from minerals, which are found in different places, generally in the rocks beneath the surface of the earth. These minerals are called ores, and most of them have special names, for there are several ores of each metal. A metal exists in its ore something in the same way as salt exists in the sea. An ore of a metal is that metal united with something else; and, to get the metal by itself, that something has to be taken away. To get salt from the sea, one has only to heat the salt-water, and boil away the water. From some ores the pure metal may be got in the same way; from others the metal can only be got by mixing, and in many cases heating, the ore with something which takes away the substance other than the metal which is in the ore. It follows, of course, that the weight of the metal got from an ore is less than the weight of the ore.

§ 16. **Iron.**—The nails and screws which are used to fasten the wooden parts of a house together are made of iron, and iron is got as follows:—There are found in the earth layers or seams of substances, called iron-ore. These contain iron-rust, and sometimes the gas carbonic acid, and sometimes clay. In order to get the metal-iron out of this mixture, the ore is mixed with limestone and coke (see § 2) or charcoal (see § 30), and put into a hollow brick tower, something like a lime-kiln, only much larger. A little way above the bottom of this tower, which is called a furnace, there is a hole through the wall, called the blast-hole. The coke at the bottom is set fire to, and air is blown in through the hole to quicken the burning. The lime and the coke together take nearly everything away from the iron, and leave it as a melted metal, which, being heavy, makes its way down to the bottom of the furnace below the hole. Some of the things which were united with the iron now unite with the coke, and rise and escape from the top of the tower as a gas; the others form, with the lime and ashes of the coke, a body which, at this high temperature, melts, and also sinks down and settles upon the melted iron. It is called SLAG, and is like melted glass; in fact, it is a kind of glass. If a hole is opened in the furnace lower than the blast-hole near the bottom of the furnace, the iron runs out; if another hole is opened above the iron, the slag runs out. As the coke itself burns away, and the slag and the metal are run off, the upper parts of the mixture of coke, limestone, and ore sink slowly down. The furnace would thus become empty. Instead of allowing this, fresh quantities of the same mixture are continually put in at the top, so that the same furnace is kept alight for many years. The iron which is thus made is called CAST-IRON; it can be melted, though not so easily as lead or tin, and it can, in the melted state, be cast in moulds made of dry sand, so as to have any form. In many houses and bridges, railway stations, and so on, beams and arches of cast-iron are used. Cast-iron is very brittle. It is not pure iron. It contains a considerable quantity of carbon, and this makes it brittle. To get it pure, it is, when it is melted, stirred up while a draught of very hot air is blown over it; then it is hammered, and squeezed, and kneaded like dough. By this means some of its impurities are squeezed out and others are burnt off. That which is burnt off is mainly carbon. The iron thus purified is called WROUGHT-IRON. It is much more tough than the cast-iron—that is, it can be bent, and remain bent, without breaking; but it is not so easy to melt. It can be rolled, when hot, into bars and rods, and rolled between rollers into sheets or plates. It is so tough that, when cold, it can be drawn through little holes, and so made into wire. It can be pressed or stamped into nails and cut into screws.

Steel will be described in § 80.

Questions.—What are the chief metals used in building? What is each used for, and why? What is an ore, and where are ores found? Why is the weight of metal which can be got from an ore always less than the weight of the ore itself? What is iron ore generally made of? How is an iron-furnace made? What is put in at the top? What is the use of the fuel? What is the use of the lime? What is slag? How is cast-iron made into wrought-iron? What is the difference between them—(1) as to what they are made of, (2) as to what they are like, (3) as to what they are used for?

VI.

Lead, Zinc, Copper, Brass, Tin, Mercury, Tin-plate, Zinc-plate, Galvanised Iron.

THINGS TO BE SEEN.—*Pieces of the metals—lead, zinc, copper, brass, tin, and mercury. Also, ores of these metals, such as sulphides of lead, zinc, and copper—oxide of tin—cinnabar—sal-ammoniac—some tin-plate—some zinc-plate.*

§ 17. **Lead.**—Lead is used in houses chiefly for water-pipes and cisterns, and for lining the gutters or roofs, and sometimes for covering roofs. Though clean bright lead easily tarnishes in the air—that is, rusts—the rust does not go very deep, and that which forms on the surface shields the metal beneath.

Lead is found in the earth united with different substances. The chief ores of lead are two. The most common one of these is a union of lead with sulphur—that is, brimstone. This ore gives up its lead, when heated, as follows:—It is first heated red-hot and stirred about, while it is exposed to plenty of air—that is, it is roasted. It is then heated more strongly, with only enough air to burn the fuel. All the sulphur is burnt off, and the melted lead remains; or the roasted ore may be heated with scraps of wrought-iron, which takes away everything else, leaving the lead.

§ 18. **Zinc** (also called SPELTER).—The chief ores of

zinc are (1) the rust of zinc united with carbonic acid, and (2) zinc united with sulphur. To get zinc from the first, it is first heated in a kiln (not a clamp) like a brick-kiln; this drives off the carbonic acid, and leaves zinc-rust. The next process is to mix the zinc-rust with fine coal-powder and a little water, and to heat it white-hot in wide earthen tubes, closed all round except at one end, where narrower open tubes are fastened on. The zinc-rust is changed into zinc, because the coal takes away that with which it is united. To get zinc from the ore which contains sulphur, the ore is first roasted—that is, it is heated in an open furnace by means of a flame playing upon it. By this means the zinc-sulphur is changed to zinc-rust, and the latter is mixed with coal and heated as above.

§ 19. **Copper.**—Copper is sometimes, but rarely, found as a metal. It is also found united with sulphur, with sulphur and iron, as copper-rust, and as copper-rust united with carbonic acid. The process of getting pure copper from its ores is a long and difficult one. If the sulphur copper-ore is worked for copper, it is first roasted; this changes the copper-sulphur into copper-rust. This is then melted and broken up, and again roasted, and so on several times. At last the copper-rust is heated with fine coal; this brings it to the state of crude copper. It is again and again broken up (by being poured into water when melted), and roasted and melted. At last, when it is nearly pure, it is covered, when melted, with charcoal, to keep out the air, and stirred up with a wooden pole. This finally purifies it by converting any copper-rust in it into copper.

§ 20. **Brass.**—Brass is a mixture of copper and zinc. The two mix when melted together, and any weight of copper will mix with any weight of zinc. So that a brass may be rich in copper and poor in zinc, or the other way about.

§ 21. **Tin.**—The ore of tin which is most useful and

abundant is tin-stone, which is rust of tin. This is crushed and washed, so as to get rid of lighter grains, which contain no tin, but sometimes other metals. The ore is then roasted, like the copper-ore, by means of which any sulphur which may be there is driven off. The ore so purified is then mixed with small coal and some slaked lime (see § 3), and strongly heated. The slaked lime takes up sand, and forms a slag, and at the same time gives up bubbles of steam, and so stirs up the tin. The coal unrusts the tin-rust, and leaves the metal itself. This is still impure. To purify it partly, it is slowly heated, and the tin, melting, first runs off, and is collected. To get it still purer, it is re-melted, and blocks of green wood are thrust beneath its surface. The heat of the melted metal causes the water in the wood to boil, and this thoroughly stirs up the tin, and brings to the surface a scum, which contains most of the impurities.

§ 22. **Mercury, or Quicksilver.**—This metal is a liquid at the ordinary temperature of the air. It is sometimes found in the metallic state as small drops in the place where mercury ores occur. The principal ore of mercury is CINNABAR, which is mercury united with sulphur. This ore is ground to powder, and mixed with quick-lime. The mixture is put into a long iron box, in one end of which is an iron tube, bent down, and dipping under water. When the ore is thus heated with the lime, the latter takes away the sulphur from the mercury, and leaves it as a metal. But at this temperature the mercury boils away as a gas, and the mercury gas meets with the water, and is so cooled that it becomes liquid—just as the steam from a kettle becomes water when it touches a cold plate held near the spout. The mercury drops through the water as a liquid metal. Very often the mercury is got by heating the cinnabar by itself, without lime.

§ 23. **Tin-plate.**—Sheet-iron covered with tin is shielded by the tin from the rusting action of air and water; so that, although tinned iron is dearer in the first place than simple iron, it lasts longer, and may be cheaper in the end. Tinned iron, or, as it is sometimes called, "tin-plate," is used for roofing instead of tiles, and for such pots and pans used in cooking as are not heated hotter than boiling water, such as kettles or stew-pans. Grid-irons, frying-pans, and pie-dishes are heated so hot that the tin would melt—for tin melts rather easily. Iron-plate—that is, sheet-iron—is covered with tin in the following way:—The sheets of iron are first thoroughly cleaned by being rubbed with dilute oil of vitriol (see § 132), sand, and water; then quickly wiped and plunged into hot melted fat. This boils away the dampness on them. They are then dipped in a pan of melted tin covered with melted fat; the tin sticks to the iron. When they are taken out of the tin bath, they are put into another grease bath, where the unnecessary tin drains off, and then they are cooled gradually.

§ 24. **Zinc-plate, or Galvanised Iron.**—There are several ways by which iron is coated with zinc. The simplest plan is to dip the perfectly clean iron plate into melted zinc, the surface of which is covered with SAL-AMMONIAC. Sal-ammoniac is a body got from the gasworks (see § 40) by adding hydrochloric acid (see § 120) to the water which has dissolved the ammonia. Sal-ammoniac is made of nitrogen, hydrogen, and chlorine.

Questions.—What is lead used for in houses, and why? What is the commonest ore of lead? How is lead got from its ore? What are the two chief ores of zinc? How is the metal got from each of them? What are the chief ores of copper? What is the use of roasting sulphur-copper ore? What is done to the roasted copper ore, and why? What is brass? What is tin-stone? What is the use of roasting the tin-stone? What is then done with the roasted ore? Why? What is the chief ore of mercury? How is mercury got from it? What is tin-plate? What is it used for? How is sheet-iron covered with tin? What is zinc-plate? What is sal-ammoniac? Where is it got from, and how?

VII.

Glue, Whitewash, Glass, Litharge, Putty.

THINGS TO BE SEEN.—*Glue—glue softened in cold water—weak solution of glue—the same after setting—chalk—whiting—pieces of different kinds of glass—emery powder—iron rust (rouge)—oxide of tin (that is, "putty powder")—litharge—linseed oil.*

§ 25. **Glue.**—The skins, horns, hoofs, or sinews of animals are stirred about for several weeks in water to which has been added enough slaked lime (see § 3) to form a milky liquid. They are then taken out and exposed to the air by being frequently turned over, and are left to dry; they are then washed and boiled with water. The liquid thus got is filtered through flannel and poured into boxes or barrels, where it becomes a jelly called SIZE. The jelly is turned out upon a table and cut into slices by a wire, and again, downwards, by a knife. The slices of jelly are placed on nets, which are hung in a dry room. The water passes off and leaves cakes of glue, which can be kept for any length of time. To use glue, it has to be broken into little pieces and covered with cold water till it is quite soft. The pot which holds it is then put into another pot in which there is some water, and the outer water is boiled. This prevents the glue from being burnt, which would happen if the inner pot were put over the flame. To stick things together with glue, the two things are covered with glue, and kept pressed together till the glue has cooled and become a jelly, and further, till the water in it has escaped into the air, leaving nothing but solid glue between the things. A mixture of plaster of Paris and glue makes, when cold and dry, a very hard cement, and is useful to fill up holes in wood, such as the holes where screws and nails have been; but such a cement will not stand water, which softens the glue, and gradually dissolves the plaster of Paris.

§ 26. **Whitewash.**—WHITING is very fine-grained CHALK, which has been cleaned. Chalk is formed much in the same way as limestone (see §§ 3, 8): it is softer and generally whiter than limestone. Whiting is made from chalk as follows:—The chalk is ground with water into a paste, and then stirred up with water and allowed partly to settle: the particles of sand which may be in the chalk, and the larger grains of chalk, settle down to the bottom first; the very fine grains of chalk remain in the water, making it milky. This milky water is put into a vat, and allowed to stand for a long time. The fine chalk-grains at last settle down, leaving the water clear. The clear water is poured away, and the soft white chalk-mud is drained and dried, and is then called whiting. If glue (see § 25) is dissolved in a large quantity of hot water and allowed to cool, it becomes a jelly called "size;" on heating the size, it melts again. Whitewash is made of melted size mixed with whiting. When the whitewash dries (that is, when the water escapes into the air), there is nothing left but grains of whiting (fine chalk) stuck together by glue; and the glue sticks itself and the whiting to the thing which is whitewashed.

§ 27. **Glass.**—There are five or six kinds of glass, which differ from one another not only in the uses to which they are put, but also in the things of which they are made, and the ways of making them. The glass of which common windows are made is got by melting together, in an earthenware pot, at a very strong heat, some sand and soda (see § 120), or potashes, or both. For crown glass, some saltpetre (see § 50) and lime (see § 3) are added. For plate glass, such as the large windows of shops, the saltpetre is sometimes left out. But almost every manufacturer uses these things in different proportions. To give the glass its proper shape and thickness for windows, an iron tube is put into the pasty melted glass, and the lump which sticks to the end is blown into a bubble, like a soap-bubble. The place opposite to the blowpipe is opened, and by turning the blowpipe round—that is, by trundling it like a mop—the hole opens, and the bubble becomes a round and flat sheet. Instead of this, the glass bubble is often blown inside a wide tube of smooth metal, so that it becomes like a garden-roller in shape; then, when still hot and soft, it is cut open by a straight cut, laid open, and flattened down. To make plate glass, the pot of glass is emptied on a metallic table, and rolled out like a pie-crust by a metal roller. It is then put in an oven and cooled very slowly, because, if it is cooled quickly, it is very brittle. Then it is ground flat with sand and water, smoothed by being ground with water and emery (see § 130) of increasing fineness, and then polished with water and iron-rust; and the polishing is finished by rubbing two plates together, a little water and rust of tin being put between them. CRYSTAL, of which salt-cellars, decanters, and "cut" glass things are generally made, contains lead-rust.

§ 28. **Putty.**—To fix windows in their frames, putty is generally used. This is made by grinding and kneading together some whiting (see § 26) and linseed oil (see § 59), which has been boiled with LITHARGE. Litharge is a rust of lead—that is, an oxide of lead. The boiling of the linseed with this body gives the oil the property of drying; so that the putty, when dry, is whiting mixed with the hard dried oil. When not in use, putty may be kept soft by covering it with water. The water does not dissolve it, but keeps away the air, which would otherwise dry the linseed oil.

Questions.—What is glue made from? How is it made? What is done to the glue when it is wanted to be used for sticking things together? How does the glue act? What is whiting? How is it made from chalk? What is size? What is common window-glass made from, and how? What is crown glass? What is plate glass? How are they made? What is crystal (glass), and what is it used for? How is plate glass polished? What is putty used for? How is it made? What is litharge? What is the use of boiling litharge with linseed oil? Why is putty kept sometimes under water?

PART II.

WHAT MATTER IS MADE OF.
ELEMENTS, AIR, FIRE, FLAME, WATER.

VIII.

Elements, Air.

THINGS TO BE SEEN.—*Pieces of iron, copper, lead, zinc, and as many other metals as can be easily got—some water, sand, sugar, and glue—some sulphur, charcoal, charcoal a little burnt, showing the ash—a thin paper bag—a bottle of soda water.*

§ 29. **Elements.**—You remember that there are twenty-six letters in the alphabet, and that every word used is either one of these letters alone ("a"), or is made by uniting two or more letters together. Think of the number of words which there are, all made of these twenty-six letters. Or think of the endless number of numbers which can be made by putting together the ten numerals, 0, 1, 2, and so on; or think of the number of tunes which can be played with twenty or thirty notes. When you have thought of this well, take up any piece of matter you please, and look upon it as a word. If it be a piece of iron, it will be like a word of one letter. If it be a drop of water, or a grain of salt or of sand (silica), it will be like a word of two letters. If it be a lump of sugar, it will be like a word of three letters. This is because, just as all words are made of letters, so all pieces of matter are made of ELEMENTS—that is, simple single kinds of matter, which can no more be divided into other kinds than a letter can, but which, like the letter "a," can stand by themselves. Iron is an element. Water is made of two elements. So is salt; but the elements in salt are neither of them the same as either of the elements of water. Silica is also made of two elements. Sugar is made of three elements, glue of four, and so on.

There are known to be sixty-six different Elements. More may hereafter be found in nature. Every kind of matter which can be got at has been examined, and has been found to be either an element itself, like gold or sulphur, or a union of two or more elements. Elements are the letters of Matter.

Not only has every known thing been examined in this way, and been proved to be made of these elements, but, by uniting together elements and compound bodies (that is, bodies themselves made up of elements), a very great number of new bodies have been made which did not before exist, just as new words may be formed out of the known letters. But while new words, unless they describe new things, are nonsense, there is no nonsense in nature, nor in the things which can be made out of matter.

Many of these elements are so rare that we seldom meet with them, and they shall not be talked of in this book. Others are so common, that we cannot understand what we are about in the world unless we know something about them. They will be described as we go on.

§ 30. **Air.**—Because the air is so soft that we can move through it easily, because we can see through it so well, and because, when pure, it has neither taste nor smell, we are apt to think that it is not there. But think of the wind, which is moving air, how it presses. Or fill a well-made paper-bag with air, and screw up its mouth and squeeze it, you find that it will not easily give in. So, though we do not see, or taste, or smell the air, and only feel it when it blows or we pass through it quickly, yet we know it is matter. But it is not like stone, which is a solid, nor like water, which is a liquid: it is a gas. Air contains and is wholly made of four gases. Two of these are elements—namely, NITROGEN and OXYGEN—and they together form by far the largest part of the air. Two of them are compounds—namely, WATER and Carbonic Acid. Water is made of oxygen and hydrogen. Carbonic acid is made of oxygen and CARBON. So that the air is made of four elements—Nitrogen, Oxygen, Hydrogen, and Carbon. Although nitrogen forms about four-fifths of the air—that is, in every five gallons of air there are four of nitrogen—yet we shall seldom have to speak about it again in this book. The gas carbonic acid is the gas which is seen to rise as bubbles when a bottle of beer, or ginger-beer, or soda-water is opened. It has a pleasant taste, a little sharp; and liquids which usually contain it are flat when it is not there. When animals breathe in and out, the air which they breathe out contains more carbonic acid than the air they draw in. Although a thousand gallons of air contain less than half-a-gallon of carbonic acid, this small quantity of carbonic acid is of the greatest importance, because it, together with water, forms the chief food for plants.

You know what CHARCOAL is like. If you bake a piece of wood for a long time at such a great heat that it nearly catches fire, but not quite, you find it changed to charcoal (charred). Charcoal is nearly pure carbon. The ash which is left when charcoal is burnt is almost the only part of the charcoal which is not carbon. This ash contains all the mineral or earthy matter which the plant has got from the earth. The whole of the carbon has been got from the air, and, of course, from that part of the air which contains carbon—namely, the carbonic acid. Thus you see how useful this small quantity of carbonic acid is; without it, plants could not grow, and therefore all animals would die; for all animals either live on plants, or on other animals which do so.

Questions.—What is an element? How many elements are there in water? How many in salt? How many in sugar? How many in glue? About how many elements are known? How do we judge air to be matter? Of what two gases is air chiefly made? How many gallons of each are there in a hundred gallons of air? What two other gases are there in the air? What elements is water made of? What elements is carbonic acid made of? In what drinks is carbonic acid found? How much carbonic acid is there in a thousand gallons of air? What about the breath of animals in regard to carbonic acid? What is charcoal? Where do plants get their carbon from? Where do plants get the stuff which is found in their ashes?

IX.

Fire.

THINGS TO BE SEEN.—*Sugar dissolving in water—charcoal burning in air—rusted iron—flint and sand.*

§ 31. **Fire.**—When charcoal is burnt, I said, nothing is left but ashes. What becomes of the carbon? Burnt away. Yes; but away where to, and how? When you put a lump of sugar into a basin of water, the sugar melts away; you can see it no more. But you know that it is there; you know that if you were to let the water dry up, you would find the sugar again. You cannot destroy matter. What happens to the carbon of the charcoal is this: it unites with the oxygen in the air, and with it forms carbonic acid, and this spreads and mixes with the air. It is a gas as colourless as air; and because you can see through it so well, you can't see it, just as by some lights you can't see a sheet of glass. The burning of the charcoal is therefore the act of its uniting with the oxygen in the air; such uniting is called *combustion*, and, more exactly, *oxidation*.

RUSTING is another common instance of oxidation. A piece of iron exposed to the air, if the air be moist, tarnishes and rusts. It slowly unites with the oxygen of the air. But the result of such union is the red-brown solid body called rust, instead of being a gas, as is the case with carbon. The carbon which has been partly burnt away of course weighs less than at first. The iron which has rusted weighs more as long as the rust sticks to it, because all the iron is there, together with oxygen. Of course if the rusted iron be cleansed from rust, it weighs less than it did at first, because then all the oxygen is taken away again, together with the iron with which it is united.

The body formed when a substance unites with oxygen is called the oxide of that substance. Thus carbonic acid is an oxide of carbon; rust of iron is an oxide of iron; flint or silica is an oxide of silicon, and so on.

Notice, that plants, while they grow, take carbon out of the carbonic acid of the air, whereas, when the carbon of plants is burnt, carbonic acid enters the air again; so that when you set fire to a thing, you set it off oxidising, and it may get far hotter than you made it. It comes to this—in order to start it burning, you must heat it with oxygen, that is, in the air. The part you start burning is, while burning, hot, and heats the rest enough to start it burning, and so on. Think how a fire spreads. Different bodies have to be heated to different degrees in the air before they catch fire; and when burning, they are not all equally hot. Even the same substance when burning may be hotter at one time than at another. The quicker any substance burns, the hotter it is while burning, but of course the sooner it is burnt out. In the one case, you have a lesser hotness for a longer time; in the other, a greater hotness for a shorter time. The one just makes up for the other. Hotness is often called "temperature." Though a coal burns when in the fire, it soon goes out when taken from the grate. The burning part throws off so much heat into the air, that it cools itself, and has no heat to spare to set fire to the rest. But two or three red-hot coals close together keep on burning at the parts facing one another, because the heat which one throws off in burning is caught by the others, and, so little heat being able to escape in this way, the heat of burning keeps the burning up. A fire is usually laid in a grate by first putting in paper, then wood on the top of the paper, and coal on the wood, the whole being so built that air can pass freely amongst it. Paper is easily set fire to, because it is so thin that it is easily heated through sufficiently hot to burn. Paper burns with a flame, and this flame laps round the wood, and heats it hot enough to set it on fire. The wood, too, burns with a flame, which enters amongst the coal, and sets fire to the faces of the coal, which, for the above-given reason, do not go out when several are facing one another. The coal itself generally burns with a flame, and this helps the fire to spread. Coke has little or no flame, and that is why it is hard to light a coke fire with wood alone, and why the fire in a grate full of coke spreads so slowly.

Questions.—What becomes of the carbon of the wood when the wood is burnt? What is burning, or combustion? What is rusting? What is rust? How is it that iron gets heavier as it rusts? What is meant by an oxide? How is it that a fire spreads? How is it that a fire burns in a grate, but a red-hot coal soon goes out if taken out of the fire? In lighting a fire, why is paper used? Why is wood used? How is it that fire spreads so slowly through coke?

X.

Fire, Flame.

THINGS TO BE SEEN.—*A burning coal fire—soot—a gas-flame (a candle-flame will do nearly as well)—a clean metal spoon—a bright table-knife—a bottle of lime-water—a tumbler—a card or plate to cover the tumbler—some vinegar.*

§ 31 *(continued)*.—A coal fire is the oxidation of coal—that is, coal being oxidised. Coal contains, and is entirely made up of the following elements:—Carbon, Oxygen, Hydrogen, Nitrogen, Sulphur, and about eight elements and metals which are found in the ash. But carbon is the chief thing in coal. Different kinds of coal contain these elements in different quantities. A hundred pounds of some kinds of coal leave as much as six pounds of ash, of others only one pound. Nobody knows how these elements are united with each other in the coal. The ash we need not care about now. The elements of the coal which burn are the carbon, hydrogen, and sulphur. The oxygen and hydrogen are united with some of the carbon as they were when the coal was wood. The sulphur is not only useless, but is a nuisance in the coal. It burns, and some of its oxide is found in the ash, some of it, incompletely burnt, goes up the chimney, and makes the air of cities where coal is burnt sour. The carbon and hydrogen are completely oxidised in a clear fire, partly by the oxygen in the coal; but as this is not nearly enough to burn them, they are burnt by the oxygen of the air which enters the grate. The carbon is burnt to carbonic acid (see § 32), and the hydrogen to water (see § 33). The nitrogen in the air and the nitrogen already in the coal rise up the chimney; so that the gases rising up the chimney from a clear burning coal fire are carbonic acid, water, nitrogen, and oxidised sulphur. All these are, at this hotness, colourless invisible gases. From most coal fires smoke arises from the upper part of the fire; this is because there is not enough air passing through the fire, and because the heat there is not strong enough; in fact, the coal is being partly distilled, as in making coke, and the visible smoke is a dense tar and particles of carbon. These collect either in the chimney or in the air, and are known as SOOT. Soot is wasted fuel.

§ 32. **Flame.**—The substances which we have been examining as givers of light all burn with a flame. If you turn down a gas-flame till it is only about an eighth of an inch long, it burns blue and gives but little light; a hundred of such little blue flames would not give enough light to read by; or if you blow, or if the wind blow pretty hard upon a gas-flame which is giving light, the flame is blown on one side, turns blue, and gives scarcely any light. In the last case, in the blue flame which gives no light, as much gas comes out of the pipe and is burnt as before it was blown, and the flame is not smaller. How is it that the one flame gives more light than the other? Put now the end of a spoon or any body which will not burn for a few seconds, first into the light-giving flame where the light is strongest, you find it covered with soot; wipe it and put it in the flame which is quite blue and gives so little light, and you will see that the spoon remains clean. And so whenever burning gas gives its yellowish-white light there is SOOT in the flame. Soot is very nearly pure carbon, and is also called LAMP-BLACK. When there is no soot, there is only the feeble blue light. Now let the gas burn so as to give its proper yellowish-white light, and hold the spoon above the flame—it remains bright. This shows that it is the hot soot which gives the yellow light, and that the soot exists only in the flame. Take the bright spoon again, or a bright table-knife blade, and let it be quite cold; hold it above the flame for a second only, and examine it instantly, and you will find it covered with a dew, as though you had breathed on it. This dew is water. This takes place however dry the air of the room is, and however dry is the coal-gas; so that this water is formed in the flame. Now take some water which has been shaken with slaked lime (see § 3) and become clear (it is called lime-water). Hold a cold dry tumbler over the gas-flame for a second or two, turn out the gas, cover the mouth of the tumbler with a sheet of cardboard, turn the tumbler and card over, pour a little of the lime-water into the tumbler, put on the card, and twirl the tumbler round. The lime-water will become milky, and the milkiness will settle down. This white substance is nothing but lime united with carbonic acid; and you can show that it contains carbonic acid by pouring off most of the liquid above it and adding a little vinegar, whereupon it will froth up. This frothing is the rising through the liquid, and escape into the air, of bubbles of carbonic acid. This carbonic acid, like the water, has been formed in the flame.

Questions.—What is coal chiefly made of? Which elements of the coal burn? What gases are formed when coal is burning? What other gas goes up the chimney? What is smoke? What is soot? How can it be shown that when coal-gas burns, water is formed? How that carbonic acid is formed? How is it that there is soot in a bright gas-flame, and none when the flame is burning blue? What becomes of the soot in a bright flame? What is lime-water? What is the milkiness which carbonic acid makes in lime-water? How would you show that this milkiness contains a gas?

XI.
Flame.

THINGS TO BE SEEN.—*A burning candle—a large drawing of a candle-flame—a tallow candle* (§ 41) *or dip—a composite or stearine candle* (§ 44)*—an air-gas burner.*

§ 32 *(continued).*—Let us now look very carefully at a candle burning steadily in a dark room. You see at the top a cup of melted tallow or stearine or paraffin, or of whatever else the candle is made. The solid is melted of course by the heat thrown off by the flame. Rising through the middle of this stands up the wick, which is still unburnt and unblackened in the liquid, and a little way above. Just where the flame begins the wick is charred black, and all the rest of the wick is black except the tip, which, if the wick is made to curl (see § 41), as most wicks are now made to do, is red-hot, and is manifestly burning away like a hot coal, leaving, however, little or no ash, because the cotton is made of little else than carbon, oxygen, and hydrogen—that is, it is a substance containing and consisting of these elements. The real purpose of the wick, however, is not to burn; for one can use metal wicks; not well, it is true, with candles where the level of the burning matter is always sinking, and which would so leave the metal sticking out too far, but with oil lamps, where the level of the burning matter can be kept pretty constant. The real purpose of the wick is to become soaked with the liquid matter (say stearine). For, like all finely fibrous or porous solids, a mass of cotton gets wetted with a liquid a good way up, when its lower part dips into that liquid. When the liquid reaches the flame, it is first simply distilled—that is, made by the heat into a vapour or gas. Any of it which cannot so rise remains on the wick. This vapour forms the inner part of the flame, and you can easily see that it is dark; in fact, there is really no flame in this part at all. Outside this is the proper light-giving part. In this part the hydrogen of the stearine is burning, water being here formed. The carbon of the stearine is therefore deprived of its hydrogen. The burning of the hydrogen gives rise to an exceedingly great heat, and this heat makes the particles of carbon white-hot. Further up in the flame, and at the sides of this light-sheath, you see a faint bluish sheath. It is here, and at the outer edge of the light-cone, that the carbon is burnt, and also at the end of the wick. The reason why dips (see § 41) with straight wicks want snuffing is that, as soon as the top of the wick finds itself in the light-flame, it gets coated with soot and swells, and so stops the gas-currents of the flame, thus making the flame still more smoky. And besides, the part of the tallow which heat cannot volatilise gathers there; whereas in the curled wick this is exposed to the hot air, and is burnt off. All through the flame, in all its parts excepting the inner parts, the nitrogen of the air is rushing. The shape of the flame is given by the upward rush of the hot gases, and the inward rush of the surrounding air.

The gas-burners called *air-gas* burners show that the

light-giving power of flames is due to the existence in them of unburnt carbon. In these burners coal-gas enters one end of a metal tube and burns at the other. But just where it enters the tube there are some holes. The upward current of the coal-gas draws air in, and this mixes with the gas, so that when they both reach the flame there is enough oxygen to burn the carbon as well as the hydrogen at once; so that there is no stage where the carbon is heated white-hot by the heat of the burning hydrogen. A common gas-burner gives out just as much heat as an air-gas burner if they both burn the same quantity of gas. But the air-gas burner's flame is not so smoky inside.

Questions.—What is the use of the wick in a candle? What happens first to the melted stuff when it creeps up to the flame? What is in the very inside of a candle flame? What is taking place in that part of the flame which gives out light? What substance is there found? What is it which gives out light? What takes place outside the light-giving part of the flame? Why do dips need snuffing? Why are plaited wicks used? What is an air-gas burner, and why is it sometimes used?

XII.

Water.

THINGS TO BE SEEN.—*A kettle of boiling muddy water—the steam from it cooled on a plate and drops of distilled water formed—a piece of porous sandstone with a hollow in it—muddy water filtered through the sandstone.*

§ 33. **Water.**—Water is a union of the gas OXYGEN with the gas HYDROGEN; it is therefore an oxide of hydrogen. Two gallons of hydrogen must have one gallon of oxygen to burn to water. A gallon of oxygen is sixteen times as heavy as a gallon of hydrogen, so that to burn to water one pound of hydrogen eight pounds of oxygen are needed. Hydrogen is not found by itself anywhere on the earth, or even mixed with other gases, as nitrogen and oxygen are in the air. Of course the vapour of water contains hydrogen, and so therefore does moist air. Marsh gas also contains hydrogen, but in this case the hydrogen is united with carbon (see § 40). Hydrogen is the lightest stuff known. The water which we find in the sea, in rivers, lakes, springs, and wells, is never quite pure. But if you hold a cold plate against the spout of a kettle of boiling water, you will get a few drops of nearly pure water. This is distilled water. You all know how the rain falls from the sky, and how the rain-water collects in little brooks and streams and rivers, how it flows down to the sea, and how the sun shining on the sea is always at work drying up the sea and raising its water to the sky from which it fell. It would be as unwise to look upon the sea as the original source of water, as it would be to look upon the sky as the original source. The hen gives rise to the egg, and the egg to the hen. Let us consider a falling rain-drop. At first it is as pure water as that which you collected on the plate from the kettle of boiling water. But as it falls through the air it absorbs a little oxygen and carbonic acid. These enable the water to eat away rocks and earths. If a rock is made up of grains of two kinds of substances, and if one of these substances dissolves out in the rain-water, the other will be left full of holes and crumbly, and so it may crumble to pieces and become mud. If the rain-water flows at once to a rapid brook, and so to a rapid river, and on to the sea, the part of the rock truly dissolved and the mud reach the sea together. The mud there settles, but the truly dissolved rock does not. If the rain-water, after reaching the earth, meets with openings in the ground or porous rocks, it becomes filtered from mud, the particles of which cannot get through the very fine holes in the rock, but the water has plenty of chance of dissolving all it can of such rocks. If, then, the water breaks out at a lower level, it is called a spring, and spring-water is generally clear and bright, but contains more dissolved rock than river-water does. There are, then, the three qualities of natural water—Rain-water, which contains no solid matter, and is called SOFT, because it feels, when rubbed between the hands, as if there were a little soap in it; River-water, which is generally muddy, and contains animal and vegetable matter drained into it from the surface of the land, and little animals which live on such matter, and some mineral matter in solution, which last makes it somewhat hard; and, lastly, Spring-water, which is clear, but generally harder than river-water. Wells are, of course, artificial springs, and the water in them is spring-water.

Questions.—What is water made of? How many pints of oxygen are needed to burn four pints of hydrogen? How many pounds of oxygen are needed to burn one pound of hydrogen? How many pounds of oxygen and how many pounds of hydrogen are there in eighteen pounds of water? How can distilled water be got from dirty water? What is a drop of rain when it reaches the earth besides water? How does rain attack rocks? What do brooks and rivers carry along besides water? What is a spring? and how does spring-water differ from river-water? How do rain-water, river-water, and spring-water differ from one another? What is meant by hard water?

XIII.

Water (continued).

THINGS TO BE SEEN.—*A lump of ice floating in a tumbler of water, showing* (1) *the dew on the outside of the glass, and* (2) *the lightness of the ice.*

§ 33 *(continued)*.—The sunshine falling on the sea and the surfaces of lakes and rivers and the moist earth, warms them, and so warms the air which touches them. The warmer the air is, the more water it takes up. The water enters the air from such surfaces in the form of gas, which you cannot see any more than you can see the air itself. Then if such warm moist air becomes cooled, as it may do by moving, as wind, to a cooler place, it can no longer keep so much water. The water separates from it in very small drops. If you are amidst such a mass of small drops, you call it a mist; if you see it from a distance, you call it a cloud. When the air between the cloud and the earth has as much water as it can hold, the drops from the cloud, when they have stuck together so as to form large drops, fall through the air as rain. But rain-drops falling from a high cloud may, if they fall through dry air, dry up and quite vanish before they reach the earth.

It often happens that the moist air is chilled so much that the water in it is not only separated out as mist, but the little drops, of which the mist is made, themselves freeze and become ice; these may stick together and reach the earth as snow. Rain-drops, again, may fall through air which is so cold that they freeze, and they then fall as hail.

Water also comes out of the air as dew and hoar-frost. You have noticed that when a red-hot poker is taken out of the fire, you cannot hold your hand very near it. It throws off its heat through the air to your hand. So the wet earth, which has got hot in the sunshine, and made the air touching it as warm and as moist as such warm air can be, throws off its heat at night through the air, so that its surface gets cooler than the air which touches it. This surface cools this air touching it, and the air in cooling must give up water, because cold air cannot hold so much water as warm, and the water thus given up lies upon the earth, and is called dew. Frozen dew is hoar frost. I do not mean that the dew is formed and then frozen, but that it freezes as it is formed.

When water freezes, it swells and gets more bulky; so that, although a piece of ice weighs just as much as the water from which it was formed, it is larger. Thus, if you take equal sizes of water and ice, the ice is the lighter; you know it floats on water. One effect of the swelling of ice as it is formed is this—water in pipes will burst them when the water freezes in them. This is generally only noticed when the thaw sets in, and the ice again becoming water can run out of the crack. When water penetrates earth, or even hard rocks, and then freezes, it forces the parts asunder and softens them. This is good for plants, which get all their food except carbon from the soil.

Questions.—What becomes of water when it is warmed with air? What takes place in warm wet air when it is cooled? What is a mist? What is a cloud? What is the cause of rain? What is snow? What is hail? How is dew formed? How is hoar-frost formed? How do you know that ice is lighter than water? Why do water-pipes burst when the water in them freezes? What happens to wet rocks when the water in them freezes? How does the breaking of rocks by frost do good to plants?

PART III.

WOOD.

XIV.

THINGS TO BE SEEN.—*As many different kinds of sprouting seed as can be got, such as acorns, horse-chestnuts, beech-nuts, which have been sprouting for about a week or a fortnight, or mustard and cress—horse-chestnuts or walnuts carefully peeled—a few young trees grown from seed, about two years old—slices of young tree-stems cut so as to show the rings of wood and the bark (failing these, have good drawings of them)—as many different kinds of wood, smoothed, as can be got.*

§ 34. **Wood.**—When an egg is kept warm from the time it is laid, a chicken is formed in it without any food reaching it from the outside. The yolk gradually takes the form of the bird, and both the yolk and the white are used up for this end. So when an acorn feels the dampness and warmth of spring, its hard shell is softened and burst by the swelling kernel. Then it is seen that the kernel is made of three things, which partly separate, two flaps and a germ. The germ divides into two branches; one rises above the earth and forms the future stem or trunk of the oak, the other enters the ground. The young plant gets its food from the two flaps which formed a part of the original seed, until it is, as it were, weaned, and able to get its own food from earth and air. To get food from the air it wants leaves; and the rising stem carries buds, which grow and open into leaves. The flaps are by this time drained dry; they wither and fall off. The root grows and sends off side roots, so that the plant gets a firmer grip of the ground as it gets taller. From the earth, mineral matter dissolved in the water, and water itself, enter the roots and rise in the stem to the leaf. By the joint working of light and the green stuff in the leaf, the leaf breaks the carbonic acid of the air, rejecting some of its oxygen, but keeping its carbon; and out of this and the mineral matter the leaf makes a liquid which has nearly the composition of wood. This liquid comes down again, and hardens into wood between the original stalk and its skin; it gives something to the skin, and makes it into young bark, which is inside the last year's bark. It gives something to the stem or trunk. A casing of new wood is thus formed every year beneath the bark, and the bark itself grows in thickness. Wood consists of carbon, oxygen, hydrogen, and some mineral matter.

§ 35. If you cut a young tree down, and flatten and smooth the stump, you will see on the outside a ring of bark, then rings of wood one within the other, and in the middle of all the rings—that is, in the middle of the tree—a little circle of pith. If the tree is ten years old, and bears fresh leaves once, and only once, a-year, you will find ten such rings of wood; and so there will be twenty if the tree is twenty years old. Thus you can tell the age of such a tree when it is cut down, unless it has decayed away and got hollow in the middle, by counting its rings of wood. If you look carefully, you will see streaks stretching across these rings, with their ends pointing towards the centre of the tree. The wood quite in the centre is pith, and is of no use to us. The wood next to the bark is new wood, and is soft; it is called sap-wood, and is of little use. The wood between the two is the firmest, and is called heart-wood. When the tree has stopped growing, it begins to decay, and the pith and heart-wood begin first. So that it should be felled for timber at a certain age, which differs for different trees. Oaks should be felled when about a hundred years old, ash and elm at about seventy, and fir at about eighty. Such wood is the best; but more wood, though of a worse kind, can be got off the same land if the trees are cut younger and oftener, being, of course, replanted. Trees should be felled either at mid-winter or in the height of summer; at both times their juices are at rest. Felled trees with their branches lopped off are called logs. If wood is to be used for building, the bark should be taken off and the trunk roughly squared; this takes off most of the sap-wood, and allows the timber to dry equally. Timber in this state is called a "balk."

§ 36. There are two chief kinds of tree the wood of which is used in buildings—Pine-wood and Leaf-wood. The pine, fir (or spruce), larch, cedar, cypress, and yew give pine-woods; their leaves are needle-shaped, hard, and smooth, and they do not all fall off in the autumn; their fruit is something like the cone of the pine or fir-tree. All these woods contain turpentine (see § 67). Such pine-wood is generally softer than leaf-wood. Its fibres are long and straight. It stands a strong pull along the fibre, but is easily crushed from end to end. It is elastic across the fibres, and recovers its shape when bent. The most common kinds of leaf-woods or hard-woods are:—Oak, ash, elm, beech, chestnut, walnut, pear, cherry, poplar, sycamore, maple; and, of foreign woods, boxwood, greenheart, ebony, teak, mahogany, rosewood, hickory.

Though pines and firs are really different trees, the wood from them both is generally called pine-wood, and, when sawn into boards, the boards are called Deals. Scaffold-poles are generally the barked stem of the larch; and ladders are made of the same sawn down the middle from end to end.

Questions.—What happens to an acorn when it sprouts? Whence does a young seedling get its first food mainly? What is the good

of a plant's roots? What is the good of its leaves? What is the use of the green stuff in leaves? Where is the new plant-stuff made, and where does the plant store it? What is wood made of? What does the top of a tree-stump look like when it is smoothed? How can you judge of the age of a tree by the look of its stump? What is pith? What is sap-wood? What is heart-wood? At what seasons should trees be felled, and why? What are logs? What are balks? What trees give pine-wood? What substance is always found in pine-woods? What are the commoner kinds of leaf-wood? How does pine-wood differ from leaf-wood?

XV.

Wood (continued.)

THINGS TO BE SEEN.—*Planks—deals—battens—joists—laths—veneer—drawing of circular saw.*

§ 37. Whatever use is to be made of the wood, it must always be seasoned—that is, dried. It is not reckoned thoroughly seasoned till it has lost about a fifth of its weight. If it is not seasoned before it is used, it warps—that is, it cracks and bends and shrinks. Timber which is to be used as balks, as for large beams of roofs or ships, only needs one seasoning, which should last between one and two years. The balks are piled in a stack in such a manner that the air can play round each one, and they are, if possible, sheltered from the rain. However well seasoned the balk may be, when it is cut up the pieces warp again a little; so they have to be again seasoned before being finished. The balk is cut up into PLANKS, DEALS, BATTENS, and so on, by a saw, sometimes by hand, sometimes by machinery. In the common saw-pit the balk is laid upon two supports called TRESSELS, one end sticking over one of the tressels. A line is marked from end to end on the top face by stretching a chalked string above it and plucking the string: it strikes against the wood and shakes off its chalk. This line is as far from the nearest face as the plank has to be thick. Then one sawyer, standing at the bottom of the pit, and the other on the balk, each laying hold of the cross handles of the long and wide saw, one of which is at each end, they saw the balk from end to end. If the pieces are between two and six inches thick and eleven inches wide, and not less than eight nor more than twenty-one feet long, they are called "planks." Such planks are used for laying down on rough ground, so that wheelbarrows may move easily. They are strong enough to bear a heavy weight in the middle, and are so used for the platforms of scaffoldings and like purposes. If the piece is only nine inches broad, and not more than four thick, it is called a "deal." When deals are less than two inches thick they are called "cut deals." If the piece be only seven inches broad and as thick as a deal, it is called a "batten." Cut deals and battens are mostly used for boards for flooring.

When large quantities of wood are to be cut, the saw is worked up and down by a steam-engine, or by the force of falling water, and the balk is pushed up against the saw by the same power.

A still quicker way of sawing the timber when one has a great water-fall, or can afford a strong steam-engine, is by use of a round saw. This is a circle of sheet steel, with saw-teeth all round its edge. It stands upright, and projects through a slit in a long firm bench. The rod or axle on which it turns is below the bench; and the part of the saw which stands above the bench must stand higher than the top face of the timber which has to be sawn through. This timber is pushed forward between uprights called guides.

After being well seasoned as balk timber, a few weeks' seasoning after sawing into planks, deals, or battens is enough. The planks are stacked one upon the other, so that their own weight prevents them from twisting. They can shrink, and because their edges are still free—that is, not nailed down—they shrink without cracking.

The larger beams of houses are generally made of pine

or fir, or of oak, chestnut, or teak. The cross pieces of floors upon which the boards are nailed, and which are called JOISTS, are of pine, and so are the boards themselves. If the floor is not to be carpeted, and if it is to be much trodden on, oak or teak is often used. Ceilings are generally made by nailing pieces of pine split into thin and narrow strips called LATHS, and covering these with plaster. Walls separating rooms on the same floor are often made in the same way.

Doors are generally made of pine; sometimes of oak or mahogany. Chairs, wooden bedsteads, tables, and sofas are generally made of beech; the better kinds of tables and sofas of oak or mahogany. Beech tables are often "VENEERED" with mahogany—that is, thin slices of the mahogany are glued on, being nicely fitted, edge to edge. Handles of doors and drawers are often of ash or beech stained black.

Questions.—What is the use of "seasoning" wood, and how is it seasoned? How are balks cut up? What are planks, deals, and battens? How is a circular saw used? Of what woods are the larger beams of houses generally made? What are joists? How are ceilings made? What is veneer? What woods are used for chairs, wooden bedsteads, tables, sofas, door handles, and drawer handles?

PART IV.

HEATING AND LIGHTING.

XVI.

Charcoal, Peat, Coal-gas.

THINGS TO BE SEEN.—*Pieces of charcoal—peat and turf—coal-gas.*

§ 38. **Charcoal.**—If wood be heated in a Still or Retort, as coal is heated when coke and coal-gas are made (see §§ 2, 40), a quantity of tar and acid liquid (wood vinegar) and other things come off, and what remains in the still or retort is wood charcoal. This body is nothing but the element carbon, along with the earthy matter of the wood. But in most countries a large quantity of charcoal is made by the partly stifled burning of the wood itself. Small logs and branches cut short are piled in a stack, and this stack is covered, excepting in one place at the top, with earth. The stack is lighted from below, and the place of the opening above is changed from time to time, so that the draught through changes its direction, and different parts of the stack are exposed in turn to the heat. The point to be kept in view is so to regulate the quantity of air which comes into the stack, that there shall be enough air to burn the resinous matter of the wood, but not enough to burn the carbon of the wood fibres. These wood fibres are made of carbon and water, and most of this water is driven off as steam.

§ 39. **Peat.**—In many places the earth is too damp or poor or shallow for trees and shrubs to grow; then the only plants found are mosses and rushes and stunted grass and such-like. These get their earth-food from the water which comes down from other places. Their dead remains gradually make a thicker and thicker layer year by year, until in some places it is as much as forty feet thick. The upper part of such a peat bed or bog is very much like the plants which now grow on it. But the further you dig down, the more coaly the peat becomes. This peat is very porous. It is cut out with a spade, and stacked to dry. It gives out less heat when burning than the same weight of coal would do. Sometimes such substance is called "turf." But turf is properly only the upper layer of a field which contains the roots of the living plants growing on it.

§ 40. **Coal-gas.**—In speaking of coal and coke, I said that when coal was heated in an iron box having a small hole in it, a lot of gas and tar came out of the hole. This gas is crude coal-gas, and is the gas used so much for lighting streets and houses, and often for warming houses, and for cooking. The gas as it comes from the box is very dirty, and has to be cleaned before being sent through the gas-pipes to the burners. Coal-gas, even when cleaned to the utmost, is a mixture of seven or eight kinds of gases. The chief of these, in quantity, are hydrogen and a gas consisting of hydrogen and carbon, called marsh-gas. This marsh-gas is also found in coal-mines, and is then called fire-damp. It is this gas which, when mixed with the air in the mine, takes fire when a light touches it, and causes dangerous explosions. Both hydrogen and marsh-gas burn in the air, and give out great heat, but scarcely any light. In one hundred gallons of coal-gas, as it generally comes from the burner, there are about eighty gallons of hydrogen and marsh-gas together, and about thirteen gallons of other gases, which either do not burn, or do not give light when burning. So that there are only about seven gallons of gas useful for giving light. There are two or three gases in the coal-gas which have this property; they are all compounds of hydrogen and carbon, but contain a larger proportion of carbon than marsh-gas does. The impurities which are taken away from the crude coal-gas before it is fit for use are tar, ammonia, sulphide of hydrogen, and sulphide of carbon. Tar is a solid, and is made of carbon, oxygen, and hydrogen; to get rid of this, the gas need only be cooled. Ammonia is a gas, consisting of nitrogen and hydrogen; it is so very soluble in water, that the coal-gas need only be passed through water to be freed from it. If the coal-gas be passed amongst an acid body, the ammonia gets fixed. The coal-gas is sometimes passed among the acid phosphate of lime, which is used as a manure. The ammonia gets fixed, and makes the manure richer. The sulphide of carbon is a liquid when by itself, but rises as a gas in large quantities in gases which it touches. To get rid of it, the coal-gas, thus cooled and washed, is passed over quick-lime, which stops the bisulphide of carbon and the sulphide of hydrogen, at the same time as it dries the gas. The so purified gas passes through tubes into large gas-holders, and from them into the mains and pipes to the gas-burners.

Questions.—What takes place when wood is heated in a still? What comes over? What is left behind? How is charcoal usually made? How is the draught of a charcoal-kiln regulated? What is charcoal made of? What is peat? What is turf? How is coal-gas made? What are the chief gases in coal-gas when it comes from the retorts? How is it cleaned from tar, from ammonia, from bisulphide of carbon?

XVII.

Candles—Tallow, Wax, Spermaceti, Stearine, Composite, Paraffin.

THINGS TO BE SEEN.—*Tallow candle—a piece of honey-comb — bees-wax — spermaceti — composite candle—paraffin.*

§ 41. **Candles—Tallow.**—The fat of sheep and kine, of which tallow is mainly made, is contained in skins so small that you need a microscope to see them; and to get the tallow out of these skins, the fat is heated by itself in a pan, so as not to burn it. The skins are thus broken, and the tallow runs together, and most of the broken skins rise to the top of the melted tallow, and are skimmed off. Then the tallow is boiled with water, which dissolves out the dirt and takes away the rest of the broken skins. The tallow is then ladled off from the dirty water below it, and allowed to cool and harden. "Dips" are made by taking a skein of cotton (see § 54), loosely twisted, to form the wick, and dipping it into the melted tallow. It is then squeezed, so as to press out the air in it, and dipped over and over again, the tallow on it having been allowed to cool and harden after each dipping. A mixture of beef fat with mutton fat makes a harder tallow than mutton fat alone; and as candles made of such a mixture are generally cast in tubes, they are called "moulds." The tubes are of pewter (a mixture of lead and tin, see § 82); the tube stands upright, and its bottom has the shape that the top of the candle is to have, there being a little hole in it for the wick to pass through. The wick is stretched down the centre of the tube, and the tallow is poured in and allowed to harden.

The wicks of most cast, that is, mould candles, are plaited instead of being twisted; the effect of this is, that as the end of the wick burns, it curls round and sticks out of the flame, and so, coming into better contact with the air, is more thoroughly burnt away. Such candles need no snuffing.

§ 42. **Wax.**—Bees gather from flowers in spring, summer, and autumn their winter food; this is honey. They store it up in cells made of wax, and this wax is not gathered from the flowers, but is made by the bee itself out of a part of the honey. The honey and the wax cells form the honeycomb. The honey having been drained and pressed out of the comb, the wax is melted and stirred with hot water, to free it from the rest of the honey and dirt. When cold and hard, it is cut into thin shavings and exposed to sunshine and air; this whitens it, and it can then be made into candles in the same way as mould candles are made.

§ 43. **Spermaceti.**—Spermaceti, of which candles are sometimes made, is found in the head of a kind of Whale. When the animal is alive and warm, the spermaceti is liquid, being dissolved in an oil called sperm oil. On cooling, after death, much of the spermaceti separates from the oil; it is strained and pressed, and boiled with wood ashes, which further cleans it from the oil. Candles are cast from it as from wax and tallow.

§ 44. **Stearine.**—There are two different things called stearine, and candles are made out of both of them. True stearine is a hard fat which forms a part of tallow, cocoa-nut oil, palm oil, and many other oils and fats. This fat contains GLYCERINE. If the glycerine is separated from it, it is still called stearine; but it ought rather to be called stearic acid. To get this stearic acid, or stearine, from the true stearine fat, the fat is heated with water and lime, by which means a kind of lime soap (see § 119) is formed. On warming this soap with almost any strong acid, the stearic acid is got. Another way is to heat the tallow or other fat very hot in a still, and blow steam into the fat. In the vessel which catches the things which come from the still, a solid cake containing stearic acid is found. If this is melted, and allowed to partly solidify in cooling, and then pressed, the other things beside the stearic acid are pressed out, and the solid stearic acid, called stearine, is left.

Composite candles are made by mixing tallow and stearine in different proportions.

§ 45. **Paraffin.**—In some places a rock is found which can be split like slate into sheets, and which holds a large quantity of tarry matter; its tarry matter has probably got into it by neighbouring coal having been heated by the natural heat of the earth along with the rock. Such rocks are called bituminous shales. When they are heated in a vessel like a gas-retort, they first give off a colourless oil called paraffin oil, and then a tarry matter, which is of a deep brown colour; from this tarry matter solid paraffin separates on cooling. It is collected in canvas bags, and squeezed as dry as possible. To purify it, it is dissolved over and over again in the colourless paraffin oil which came over when the shale was first heated, and most of this being distilled off, the paraffin is allowed to solidify out; or it is boiled with oil of vitriol (see § 127), and then with soda (see § 120), and then with charred bones; this purifies it and makes it white. When candles are made out of paraffin, the paraffin is usually mixed with a little stearine.

Questions.—How is tallow got from fat? How are dips made? How are mould candles made? What is the use of plaiting the wick of a candle? How is bees-wax made? How is it cleaned? How is it whitened? Where is spermaceti found? How is it cleaned from sperm oil? How is it further cleaned? What is stearine, and where is it found? What is the difference between true stearine and stearic acid? In what ways are stearic acid and glycerine got from fat? What are composite candles made of? Where is paraffin found? What is bituminous shale? How is solid paraffin got from it? How is solid paraffin cleaned?

XVIII.

Oils—Mineral Oils, Animal Oils, Vegetable Oils.

THINGS TO BE SEEN—*Some petroleum, train oil, colza oil, and olive oil—sulphur—iron-pyrites—the sulphides of other metals, as many as can be got.*

§ 46. **Oils**—PETROLEUM.—As stated above, paraffin oil is the oil which first comes from the still or retort when bituminous shale is heated. Such heating often takes place in the earth itself, and the oil is found in the porous rocks themselves. Then we have only to dig wells, and the oil collects in them, like water in a water-well.

Where it is thus found in nature, it is called, generally, petroleum. The crude paraffin is often re-distilled, and the part which first comes over is kept separate from that which comes over last. The first is useful where one wants a liquid which dries up quickly, but it is dangerous to use in lamps, because it mixes as a gas with the air, and the mixture easily catches fire; the second is safer.

§ 47. **Animal Oils**—TRAIN OIL.—The fat of whales, which is called blubber, is cut into pieces and put into casks; after a time the little skins which hold the oil break and rot. The stuff is then heated and drained, and the oil which drains off is called train oil. SEAL OIL and PORPOISE OIL are got from these animals in the same way. SPERM OIL is the oil which is pressed from the spermaceti (see § 43).

§ 48. **Vegetable Oils.**—Most seeds contain oils; those most used for giving light are COLZA OIL, COCOA-NUT OIL, and OLIVE OIL. The colza is a kind of cabbage. Its seeds, when pressed, give out their oil. Cocoa-nut oil is used for lighting in the hot countries where the cocoa-nut grows, for such countries are so hot that there the oil is generally liquid. But in colder countries it becomes a soft solid, like butter, and is too soft for candles, but not liquid enough for lamps. Olive oil is not much used in this country for lighting; neither it nor cocoa-nut oil give anything like so bright a flame as colza oil.

§ 49. **Matches.**—To understand how matches are made, and how they light, it is well to understand first what are sulphur (brimstone), phosphorus, and nitre (saltpetre).

Sulphur, or brimstone, is an element; it is found by itself in large quantities in Sicily and Iceland, and other countries where there are or have been volcanoes. To free such sulphur from the rocks with which it is mixed, the rock containing the sulphur is heated in an earthenware pot having a wide tube bent down and dipping under water. On heating the pot, the sulphur melts and distils over, and is cooled and solidified by the water. It is then melted and cast in moulds, and we get it so as stick-sulphur; or it is again melted and distilled in a large, cool room. It settles on the walls and on cloths hung up in the room as a fine powder. This is collected and sold as flour of sulphur (called also flowers of sulphur). Sulphur, when heated in the air, burns (that is, it is oxidised) with a blue flame, and gives rise to a suffocating gas called sulphurous acid. This gas is sulphur not fully oxidised. The gas can be made to unite, in the presence of water, with half as much again of oxygen, and becomes then (in union with water) oil of vitriol or sulphuric acid (see § 127). Metals united with sulphur are called sulphides or pyrites.

Impure sulphur is also got from iron-pyrites (sulphide of iron), which, on being heated, gives up half its sulphur. This is impure, because it almost always contains arsenic.

Questions.—How is petroleum made in the earth? What is done to natural petroleum so as to separate the drying from the not-drying part? What is train oil got from, and how is it got? From what animals is train oil got? What is sperm oil? What are colza oil, cocoa-nut oil, olive oil? What is sulphur or brimstone? Where is it found? How is stick-sulphur got? How is flour of sulphur got? What happens to sulphur when it burns? What acid is made by further burning sulphur? What name is given to metals united with sulphur? From what other body is sulphur got?

XIX.

Matches, Phosphorus, Nitre, Nitrate of Soda, Chlorate of Potash.

THINGS TO BE SEEN.—*Some phosphorus in water in a bottle—some bone-ash, charcoal, nitre, nitrate of soda, chloride of potassium, chlorate of potash, gum arabic, paraffin, litharge, glass powder—some red phosphorus.*

§ 50. **Phosphorus, Nitre, Saltpetre.**—Phosphorus is an element, but is never found by itself in nature, because it oxidises very readily, and, indeed, often takes fire by itself when exposed to the air. It is got from the ashes of bones, in which it exists in union with oxygen (forming phosphoric acid) and lime, forming altogether a body called the phosphate of lime. The rest of the bone-ash is almost wholly carbonate of lime. This bone-ash is mixed with water and sulphuric acid (see § 127). The sulphuric acid takes the lime from both the carbonate and the phosphate, forming in both cases the insoluble body sulphate of lime (plaster of Paris, gypsum, § 12). The carbonic acid rises as bubbles, and escapes; the phosphoric acid remains in solution, and is poured off from the gypsum. It is then heated, to drive off most of the water, until it becomes thick; then it is mixed with charcoal powder and heated in an earthenware pot having a copper tube dipping under water. The carbon takes away the oxygen from the phosphoric acid and passes off as a gas (carbonic acid). The phosphorus thus left alone distils over and falls through the water; it is cleaned by being pressed under water through a bag of wash-leather, and must be always kept under water. It is a dangerous thing to make, and dangerous to touch, because it catches fire if warmed by the hand in the air, and the burns it makes are very difficult to heal. Phosphorus is, when pure, transparent and colourless, and is as soft as wax. If it be dried and heated for some time by itself, shut off from the air, it becomes hard and red, and difficult to melt, and much more difficult than before to burn. It is then called red phosphorus, or amorphous phosphorus.

Nitre (saltpetre, nitrate of potash).—Animal and vegetable matter containing nitrogen, when mixed with earth and slaked lime and carbonate of potash, and exposed for some weeks to moist air, has its nitrogen oxidised to nitric acid, which unites with the potash and lime, forming nitrates of potash and nitrates of lime. Both of these can be dissolved by water, and on adding more carbonate of potash to the solution, all the lime is made insoluble as carbonate of lime, while the whole of the nitric acid is now united with potash, and can be got pure by driving off the water by heat. It is then called nitre, or saltpetre; or, if it has been melted, whereby it is by no means altered, it is called sal-prunella. Nitre is made of nitrogen, oxygen, and the metal potassium. In parts of South America where no rain falls, the ground is covered with NITRATE OF SODA, called also, from the shape of its crystals, cubic nitre. If this be dissolved and mixed with a solution of chloride of potassium, common salt (which is chloride of sodium) is formed, and nitrate of potassium. The latter is more soluble than the former in hot water, so that, on boiling off the water from the mixture, the common salt can be scooped out as it is separated. The chloride of potassium which is used for this purpose is sometimes found as a mineral by itself, and sometimes united with chloride of magnesium, which latter, being far more soluable in water, can be dissolved out. Nitrate of potash, or nitre, contains a very large quantity of oxygen, which it readily gives up when heated, and so is used to oxidise bodies.

§ 51. **Chlorate of Potassium.**—This body, which is used in making matches, is very like nitre in most of its properties. It would take too long to describe how it is made. It is made of chlorine, oxygen, and potassium.

§ 52. **Matches,** or lucifer matches, or lucifers, as they are called, are now made chiefly of three kinds—those which have sulphur in them (these are mostly foreign); those which are without sulphur, and light when rubbed on anything which is rough and dry; and those which light easily only when rubbed on a particular surface—the last kind are called safety-matches. Sulphur matches are made by dipping the ends of splinters of wood into sulphur, and then into a paste of phosphorus, gum arabic (see § 139), and water, and some colour, such as

Prussian blue (see §§ 62, 126); the matches are then dried.

Ordinary matches without sulphur are made by slightly charring the end of the wood, then dipping it into melted paraffin (see § 45), and then into a paste of phosphorus (see § 50), nitre (see § 50), melted glue (see § 25), and an oxide of lead, and some powdered glass stained variously.

Matches which only light easily on a prepared surface are made as in the above paragraph, with the exception that the paste contains no phosphorus, but sulphur, united with antimony and some chlorate of potash. The phosphorus, instead of being as ordinary phosphorus on the match, is finely powdered red phosphorus (see § 50) mixed with fine sand, and stuck by means of glue on paper, which is generally pasted on the match-box.

Questions.—What is bone-ash? What happens when bone-ash and sulphuric acid are mixed together? How is phosphorus got from phosphoric acid? What is phosphorus like? How is red or amorphous phosphorus made? How is nitre made? What is it made of? Where is nitrate of sodium found? How is nitrate of sodium used to make nitre? What elements are there in chlorate of potash? How are sulphur matches made? How are those matches made which have no sulphur, and which light when rubbed on anything rough? How are those matches made which only light easily on certain surfaces? What are those surfaces covered with?

XX.

Lighting a Match, or Striking a Light.

THINGS TO BE SEEN.—*A flint and steel—a clean plate—a pinch of gunpowder—a magnet—a splinter of wood tipped with sulphur—some German tinder—as many different kinds of matches as can be got—"Safety" matches.*

§ 53. **The lighting of a match,** or **striking a light.**—If you hit a piece of steel upon a flint-stone you get sparks, and if you do so over a clean plate, you will see that where the sparks have fallen there are little black specks, which will cling to a magnet. These are an oxide of iron. The blow has done two things: it has torn off a little piece of the iron, and it has heated that little piece so hot that it burns in the air—that is, oxidises. Such sparks will set fire to gunpowder, and formerly guns were fired by means of flint-locks—that is, flints fastened to a bent spring, and which, on the spring being let go, struck against a piece of steel, the spark so made being thrown upon a pinch of gunpowder in the "pan," a shallow hollow outside the barrel, but leading into it through the "touch-hole." Such sparks will also set fire to rag-charcoal, called tinder, or to the dry fungus called German tinder. These substances do not burn with a flame, but smoulder. On blowing, this smouldering increases; and then, if a splinter of wood tipped with sulphur is made to touch the burning tinder, the sulphur catches fire and sets fire to the wood; and this used to be the way (which is still sometimes used) for getting a light. The cause of light, observe, was the blow. You have also noticed that when you rub two things together they get hot, and the harder you work the hotter they get; in fact, if you set yourself to do such a piece of work as pushing a wheelbarrow up a hill, you know it is harder to do this job when the axle is dry than when it is greased; you also know that if the axle is dry you find it hot at the end of the task. When you have got the wheelbarrow to the top, you are more tired if the axle is dry than if it is greased; you have done more work than you bargained for. You have not only done the work you set yourself, but you have heated the axle. So whenever you spend work on rubbing two things together, you make the things hot. FRICTION always makes things hot. It is thus when the end of a match is rubbed on a rough surface: the phosphorus, which is covered with gum or glue, is laid bare and heated; it catches fire, and immediately takes oxygen not only from the air, but from the nitre or chlorate of potash, which is touching it on the match's end. Its burning is thus helped; the whole gets hot enough to set fire to the sulphur or paraffin which is next to the wood, and so to the wood itself.

In safety-matches, where the phosphorus (see § 50), mixed with sand, is on a paper by itself, the heat of rubbing sets fire to a very small patch indeed of the phosphorus; but small as this is, the heat of its burning is enough to make the sulphur on the match-end take oxygen from the chlorate of potash there, and burn and set fire to the wood.

Questions.—What happens when you hit a piece of steel with a flint? What are the sparks so got? How can such sparks be used for getting a light? What happens when you rub any two things together? What becomes of the extra work you have to do when part of your work is lost by friction? How does a common match catch fire when rubbed? How are safety-matches made and used?

PART V.

FINISHING AND FURNISHING.

XXI.

Cotton Wadding, Thread, Warp, Woof, Muslin, Flax, Linen, Tow, Hemp.

THINGS TO BE SEEN.—*Some cotton-wool—either a pod of cotton-wool or a drawing of one—wadding—cotton yarn—cotton-thread—calico—muslin—some linseed—either a flax-plant or a drawing of one—some linen—some tow—canvas—either a hemp-plant or a drawing of one—cords or ropes of hemp—a drawing of a loom.*

§ 54. **Cotton, Calico, Muslin.**—In the southern parts of North America, in India, in Egypt, and other hot countries, a plant grows called the cotton-plant, which is a kind of mallow. But the fruit of this plant, when ripe, is a thin hard shell containing cotton-wool, and amongst this wool are the true seed. If you liken the cotton-fruit to an orange, the hard skin is to be likened to the soft skin of the orange, the cotton-wool to the pulp which we eat, and the cotton-seed to the orange-pips. The wool is picked out from the hard shell, and the seeds are torn from the wool by a machine called a gin, which is a sort of round saw, the teeth of which drag the cotton away from the seed. WADDING is the form in which cotton-wool is often sold. It is made by covering the two sides of a layer of cotton-wool with thin glue or size. COTTON-THREAD.—The cotton-wool is next carded—that is, combed—so that all the fibres lie side by side, and not across one another in a tangle. It is then drawn together, and slightly twisted, and wound on reels; from these it is again reeled off and twisted, and so forms cotton-thread. Cotton-thread for sewing is made by twisting a few of these threads together. Cotton-cloth, or calico, is made by stretching a number of such threads side by side till they form a sheet as wide as the cloth is to be. These form the WARP. Then a thread is passed backwards and forwards across them, over the first, under the second, over the third, and so on to the last. Suppose it goes over the last, it comes round, turning under the last, over last but one, and so on till it comes back to the first. It goes under this, turns round, and goes on again as it did at starting. This thread which goes backwards and forwards forms the WOOF. The woof thread is carried backwards and forwards on a reel with pointed ends called a SHUTTLE. Instead of making the shuttle move up and down as it threads its way from one side of the warp to the other, it may go straight, if, when it is going one way, the second, fourth, sixth, and so on, threads of the warp are raised; for then the shuttle goes under all these, while it goes over the first, third, and so on. When it is coming back, the second, fourth, sixth warp threads are lowered, and the first, third, fifth, and so on are raised, so that now it passes over the first lot and under the second lot. The warp threads are upon a very large reel, and each thread, just in front of the path of the shuttle, passes through a noose of varnished (see § 67) worsted (see § 70) yarn. These nooses are so fixed, that while the one half of them—say those through which the second, fourth, sixth, and so on threads of the warp pass—are raised, the other half—namely, those through which the first, third, fifth, and so on threads pass—are lowered. Then the shuttle passes; then the first set are lowered and the second raised, and the shuttle passes back. The web of calico—that is, the sheet already made—is pulled a little way from the reel as the woof thread goes backwards and forwards, so as to pull a little more warp-thread off it. By this means a continuous piece of calico many yards long is woven on a machine or loom only a few feet long. MUSLIN is a fine cotton.

§ 55. **Flax**—LINEN.—The flax-plant is a plant which dies after it has borne seed; and this it does only once a year, so it is called an annual. The seed of flax is linseed, and this seed contains the oil called linseed oil (see § 59). When the plants have done growing, they are about three feet high. They are then pulled up by the roots, and sometimes piled together lightly, so that the sun and air can get at them and dry them. In some countries this drying does not take place. Whether dried or not, the seed is beaten out, and the stems are steeped in water for a week or longer: the warmer the water the shorter is the time needed. Soft water (see § 33) is the best. The flax stem contains long threads or fibres, and these are the useful part of the plant; these fibres surround the woody part of the stem. Neither the woody part nor the resin which is in it are of any use in making linen. The soaking in the water rots the woody part and makes it brittle, but it does not injure the fibre. The soaked flax is next dried, either in the air or in drying-rooms. To get rid of the rotted wood and the resin, which have become brittle, the flax is next well beaten, rubbed, and bent about by blows with wooden hammers, or by passing it between rollers. The wood and resin, and some of the shorter fibres, are beaten out, while the best, that is, the longest, fibres remain together. The shorter fibres are shaken and combed as free as possible from the dirt, and form what is called Tow. Such tow is very coarse, and is used for making such things as sacks. The longer fibres are next combed, which again takes out the shorter fibres and bundles of fibres which are still sticking together. This is a finer tow than the first, and when woven it is called CANVAS. It is used for tents, sails, and such things. But the web which is made from hemp, which is a different plant, is also called canvas (see § 56). The spinning of the flax into threads, and the weaving of linen from it, are so like the spinning and weaving of cotton, that I need say nothing about them (see § 54).

§ 56. **Hemp.**—The plant of which hemp is made is not much grown in this country. Most of the hemp used is brought from Russia, Italy, and the East Indian Islands. It is made from the plant, which grows five or six feet high, much as flax is made from the flax-plant. The fibre of hemp is coarser and stronger than that of flax. It is used for rough towels, and especially for cords, ropes, and ship's cables; for it does not rot in the water.

Questions.—Where does the cotton-plant grow? What part of the plant is the cotton? How is the cotton-wool freed from the seed? How is wadding made? What does carding do to the wool? How is cotton-thread made from carded wool? What is the warp? What is the woof? How is the woof-thread woven into the warp? What is linen made from? What is the seed of flax? What is done to the flax-plant to get the fibres clean? What is tow, and what is it used for? What is hemp, and what is it used for?

XXII.

Paper.

THINGS TO BE SEEN.—*Calico—linen—straw—wood—hemp—tow—esparto—soda—slaked lime—chloride of lime—pieces of felt—blotting paper—size—drawing of a paper mill—resin—alum.*

§ 57. **Paper.**—A piece of paper is a sheet of fibres matted together; and paper can be made out of almost anything which has fibres. It is generally made out of cotton, linen, straw, wood, hemp, or tow, or the stalk of a sedge called ESPARTO, which grows in Spain and North Africa. When made out of cotton or linen, rags of these substances are generally used, because they are cheaper.

The dry rags are cleaned first by hand. Pins and buttons and such things are taken off. The seams are undone, and the rags are cut into small pieces and sorted. Then they are rubbed together upon a metal sieve, which frees them from dust. Next they are boiled with water, to which is added some soda (see § 120) and slaked lime (see § 3). This takes out grease and most stains. After being washed, they are torn to pieces by being brought between two sets of steel teeth, something like saw teeth. One of these sets is on a wheel which is driven round. Then, if necessary, the rags are bleached—that is, made as white as they can be. This is done by mixing them with water containing some chloride of lime (see § 131). After being again washed, they are further torn to pieces in water by an engine with saw teeth like the first one, only the teeth are finer, and the two faces which carry the teeth are nearer together. This grinds the rags into a pulp. The fibres are broken very short; all this is done by engines. The paper is made from the pulp, sometimes by hand and sometimes by machinery. Let us suppose it is to be made by hand. The pulp is kept well stirred up in a vat; into this a sieve is dipped and brought up again, care being taken not to tilt it; the water drains through the sieve and leaves a sheet of pulp, and this is helped by gently shaking the sieve. The sieves used in paper-making are made of brass wire; these are stretched in a frame side by side, close to one another, and there are a few cross wires to support the others. This frame is surrounded by an edge or rim, which can be taken off. The thickness of the paper, it is clear, is greater the deeper this rim is, and of course, also, the thicker the pulp is—that is, the less water there is in it. When the water is drained off, the rim is taken off the frame, and this is turned over on a piece of felt (see § 87), whereby the pulp which was on the frame is left on the felt; another piece of felt is now put over the paper, then another sheet of the paper, then another piece of felt, and so on. The pile made in this way is strongly pressed, so as to squeeze out as much water as possible. Then the sheets are taken out from between the felts and dried. In this state the paper is blotting-paper. Writing-ink soaks and spreads in it, and so it cannot be used for writing on. To give it the power of keeping the ink in one place, it is dipped in clean white size (see § 25), and again pressed and dried. The surface is now rough. If it be wanted smooth, the sheet is put between two very smooth sheets of copper, and the whole three are passed between two heavy metal cylinders, with scarcely enough space between them to let the copper plates and paper pass. After two or three passages through the rollers, the paper is found to have a very smooth surface, which makes it easier to write on. By far the larger quantity of paper is made from the pulp by machinery. The things which the machine does to the pulp are like those done when the paper is made by hand; but the work goes on at a greater rate. The pulp is let flow over the edge of a trough as wide as the paper is to be, and let fall upon a wire cloth, the two end edges of which are joined together. This wire cloth, in the shape of a jack-towel, passes round two rollers at the same height from the ground, so that when these rollers turn round, the upper half of the wire cloth moves away from the falling pulp. By this means, as the water drains off, a continuous sheet of partly dry pulp is carried along. Moving straps at the side stop the pulp from flowing over, and the wire sieve jerks a little sideways to help the water to run through. In order to get rid of still more of the water, the wire web carrying the pulp is made to pass closely over some boxes without tops, and the air being drawn from these boxes, the water from the pulp follows it. The sheet, thus well drained, is next passed between two rollers (like mangle-rollers) covered with felt. Then it is carried along on a broad felt band, which is in shape like the wire sieve. It passes between smooth metal rollers, which squeezes more water out, and at last over several smooth, large, hollow, metal rollers, which are made hot by passing steam through them inside. From the drying rollers it may be at once wound upon the reel, and sized afterwards, or it may be passed through the size, and again dried and pressed between rollers. For the commoner kinds of paper, such as wall-paper and brown packing-paper, a so-called size is made by dissolving together resin (see § 67), soda (see § 120), and a little alum. Sometimes the size is mixed with the pulp.

§ 58. **Straw, Esparto, and Wood Paper.**—Esparto is a kind of sedge growing in South Spain and North Africa. The plant is pulled, and dried in the sun. The wood, when used for paper-making, is sometimes torn into shreds by rough grindstones. The paper made from these substances is brittle, but their pulp, when mixed with linen or cotton-pulp, gives stiffness to the paper, and this, together with its cheapness, is why it is used for wall-papers.

Questions.—What is paper made from? How are rags cleaned for making paper? How are rags made into a pulp? How can a sheet of moist pulp be got? How is the pulp dried? What is done to blotting-paper to stop ink from spreading? How is the paper smoothed? How are wall-papers sized.

XXIII.

Paints, Linseed Oil, White Lead, Zinc-white.

THINGS TO BE SEEN.—*Linseed—linseed meal—linseed oil—oil of turpentine—litharge—sugar of lead—white lead—vinegar—tan—zinc—oxide of zinc—arsenite of copper—oxide of chromium—iron-rust—some oil-cloth.*

§ 59. **Paints and other Colours.**—The plaster, mortar, wood, or iron on the outside of houses, and the wood inside the houses, is often painted, so that the weather cannot act upon it outside, and so that it can, when inside, be made to look like stone or a different kind of wood, and be easily cleaned. Paint for such purposes is generally made of LINSEED OIL, oil of turpentine (see § 67), and some white or coloured powder, according to the colour of the paint which is wanted. The seed of the flax of which linen is made (see § 55) is linseed; these seeds, when ripe, are very slippery, and could not easily be ground. They are therefore first bruised; and this is done by letting them fall between two strong metal rollers, which have ridges on them, and which are very close together, and turn round. The bruised seed is then spread upon the bottom of a ring-shaped trough having a hard bottom, and a heavy granite roller is made to roll round the trough. This crushes the seed into a sort of flour or meal, called linseed meal, which is sometimes used for poultices. The linseed meal is then put into strong bags, warmed, and then pressed very much, so that the oil is squeezed out. If the meal be heated before being pressed, more oil is got, but it is not quite so good. The mass from which the oil has been squeezed is called oil-cake, and is very useful for fattening cattle. This linseed oil cannot be used at once for making paint, because it does not dry; but if it be boiled for a short time, or allowed to stand, with frequent shakings, for a longer time, with a little lead-rust (oxide of lead, litharge) and sugar of lead (acetate of lead, got by dissolving litharge in vinegar), it gets the power of drying in a few hours.

White paint is generally made by mixing linseed oil with WHITE LEAD and oil of turpentine (see § 67); and white lead is made as follows:—The metal lead is cast into forms like a gridiron. The lead is put on the top of earthen pots in which there is some vinegar. The pots and lead are covered loosely with boards, and on the top of these is put some old tan which has been used for tanning leather (see § 97). Another set of vinegar-pots stands on these, then more lead, planks, and tan, and so on, until a high pile is made. In two or three months the pile is unbuilt, and the lead is found to be almost all changed into a white brittle substance, called white lead. This white lead is found to be made of lead and oxygen and water and carbonic acid. The oxygen and the water it has got from the moist air. The carbonic acid has been got from the fermenting tan (see §§ 106, 115). The vinegar vapour has helped the lead to rust or oxidise, I do not know how.

The white lead is broken and scraped away from any unchanged lead, and ground with water to a kind of milk. On standing, the coarser grains settle first; those which settle last are the smallest (compare § 26); the coarser are ground again. The white mud is scooped out, drained, and dried. This, when ground with boiled linseed oil and mixed with oil of turpentine (see § 67), is white paint.

§ 60. **Zinc-white** is often used instead of white lead. It is the rust or oxide of zinc, and is therefore to be got by burning zinc. Zinc, on being heated, melts, and then, on being heated very hot indeed, boils just as melted ice, that is, water, does. When the vapour of zinc meets with the air at this very great hotness it quickly oxidises or burns, and its oxide is a white powder, called zinc-white.

Most coloured paints used for house-painting are lead—or zinc—paint mixed with coloured powder. Green paints are generally so coloured by mixing with the white paint bodies containing copper, arsenic, or chromium. Iron-rusts (that is, oxides) of different kinds and in different quantities give yellows, browns, and blacks. Black paints are also made by using the powder of some kinds of coal which contain silica. The colours of most woods and stones are like one or other of these in colour. As oil of turpentine smells badly, impure spirits of wine, called methylated spirit, is sometimes used instead of it to mix with the linseed oil and white lead.

§ 61. **Oil-cloth.**—Oil-cloth is canvas or hempen cloth, one side of which has been painted in oil colours.

Questions.—Why and on what is paint used? What is paint made of? What is linseed oil? How is it got? What is oil-cake? How is linseed oil made to dry? How is white lead made, and what is it made of? How is white paint made? How are green paints made? How are yellow, brown, and black paints made? What can be used instead of turpentine in making paints? What is oil-cloth?

XXIV.

Colours of Wall-papers, Cane, Rushes, Wicker, Horse-hair.

THINGS TO BE SEEN.—*Pipe-clay—size—whiting—Prussian blue—verditer—ultramarine (artificial)—chrome-yellow—Brazil wood—arsenite of copper—umber—cane—rushes—willow and wicker—horses' hair and webs of horse-hair.*

§ 62. **Colours of Wall-papers.**—The paper having been made in long rolls (according to § 57), and very well sized, is laid upon a table and brushed over with a mixture of white clay (china-clay, pipe-clay) and size. Generally, wall-papers are first coloured all over, or tinted, before the pattern is given to them. The colours wanted are in such cases mixed with the white clay and size. The colours used to this end are usually what are called "lake" colours—that is, the colouring-matter is in union with the earth alumina. Alumina is the oxide of the metal aluminum. After hanging up to dry, the paper is laid upon a hard smooth table with the clayed face down, and the upper face is rubbed with a smooth brass brightener. The coloured patterns are stamped upon the paper by a wooden block of the shape of the pattern, and which has been dipped in the coloured liquid. If a pattern has twelve colours, twelve blocks of the shape of the outline of the pattern are used; but the wood of each block is so cut away that only that part is left to touch the paper where a certain colour is required. By this means only one colour is used on each block. The colours used in paper-staining are very numerous. White is usually whiting (see § 26). Blue is PRUSSIAN BLUE, that is, a body made of iron, carbon, nitrogen (see § 126); or else VERDITER, which is a mixture of oxide of copper and lime, or else ULTRAMARINE, a mixture of a great many things, and which is made so as to be, in colour and in the things of which it is made, like a natural mineral of the same name, which is rare and dear. Yellow colours are often got by boiling the berries of the "dyer's weed" or "weld." Chrome-yellow is a substance made of oxygen and the two metals chromium and lead. Reds are got by boiling Brazil wood with water; the tree grows in Brazil, in the West Indies, and in Japan. Greens usually contain copper, or copper and arsenic. A mixture of Prussian-blue and chrome-yellow also gives a green. Brown colours are the natural mixtures of oxide of iron and manganese with clay, and are called umber. Most other shades are got by mixing two or more of the above colours in different proportions. Wall-papers coloured with arsenic are poisonous.

As most furniture is made of wood, and as the different kinds of wood have been already described (see § 34), there is not much left to be said about such furniture as is made of wood.

§ 63. **Cane.**—The seats of chairs are often made of cane. This cane, which is really the stem of a kind of palm, grows in Borneo and the neighbouring islands. It is simply split, and then, being woven across the frame of the chair, forms the seat.

§ 64. **Rushes.**—The common rush (not the bulrush), which grows in marshy places, is sometimes used for chair-bottoms. Such chair-bottoms are soft, but difficult to clean.

§ 65. **Wicker.**—Chairs are often made entirely of wicker; and it is of this that common baskets, such as clothes-baskets, are made. Wicker is the small branch of the willow-tree, or the sprout of the young willow-plant; the latter is usually called osier. Osier-beds are nurseries of young willows. After these are cut, they are stacked for a time, and then drawn from end to end between two knife-blades fastened in the ground, which cross one another like the blades of a partly-opened pair of scissors. The bark of the willow is thus stripped off, and the wicker is ready to be worked into baskets. Sometimes the bark is left on; it is so left in fish-baskets.

§ 66. **Horse-hair.**—Horse-hair web is simply the web made from the hair of horses' manes and tails. It is used for covering sofas and chair-bottoms, being then stretched over some stuffing. Very often so-called horse-hair webs are only half horse-hair, that is, the warp is horse-hair, but the woof is cotton or worsted. Horse-hair is also used for stuffing mattresses, and for sieves (see § 95).

Questions.—What is first done to paper in order to make wall-paper of it? What are "lake" colours? How are the colours given to the paper? What is the white of wall-papers made of? What is the blue made of? What is "verditer"? What is "ultramarine"? What are yellows made of? What are reds made from? What are greens made of? What are browns made of? What is cane? What is rush? What is wicker? What is osier? How is osier made ready for use as wicker? How is horse-hair web made, and what is it used for?

XXV.

Varnish, Turpentine, Magnesia, Resin, Shell-lac, Spirits of Wine, Lacquer.

THINGS TO BE SEEN.—*Varnish—linseed oil—gum copal—oil of turpentine—magnesia—raw turpentine—rosin—size—shell-lac—spirits of wine.*

§ 67. **Varnish.**—The varnish generally used for wood in houses is a mixture of drying linseed oil (see § 59), gum copal, and oil of turpentine (called also spirits of turpentine, or simply turpentine—see § 36). The linseed oil is made into drying linseed oil by boiling it with a little

MAGNESIA. Magnesia is the rust or oxide of the metal magnesium, and is got by heating the natural carbonate of magnesia, just as quick-lime is got by heating limestone (see § 3). After settling, the oil is ready for making varnish. GUM COPAL is a kind of resin, which is produced by some trees growing both in the East and West Indies. Turpentine is formed in European trees of the nature of pine-trees and fir-trees. Holes are cut into the wood of such trees a little above the ground, and the turpentine collects in the holes. When fresh, it is a thick colourless liquid, which hardens after a time in the air, and then is like old honey. If turpentine be boiled with water in a still, water and an oil come over together, the oil floating on the water. The oil is called OIL OF TURPENTINE, or spirit of turpentine, or turpentine, or turps. The substance which remains in the still is called RESIN, or ROSIN. Varnish is made out of linseed oil, copal, and oil of turpentine, as follows:—The copal is melted over a fire in a copper pan, but not over-heated. Hot linseed oil is stirred in, and mixes with the copal; the two are gently boiled together, and the oil of turpentine is added in small quantities at a time, and stirred in.

If varnish be applied directly to wood, a great deal of it sinks into the wood and is lost. To prevent this, the wood is first brushed over with size (that is, thin glue, see § 25). This stops up the pores of the wood, and is not washed away by the varnish.

§ 68. **French Polish.**—This is used for the finer kinds of woodwork. It is made by dissolving SHELL-LAC in spirits of wine. Shell-lac is got as follows:—In the East Indies, in Assam, and Siam, there are certain trees which are kinds of fig-trees. The twigs of these trees are sometimes pricked by little insects, and the juice which comes out hardens and coats the twig. When this hard stuff, which is a resin, is melted, and squeezed through a cloth to cleanse it, and allowed to fall on a cool substance to harden it, it is called shell-lac. If wine or beer (see

§ 115), or other liquid which has been fermented (see § 115), is heated till it boils, and if the part which boils away first as a gas is cooled, and so collected, it is found to contain a liquid called SPIRIT OF WINE, which contains carbon, oxygen, and hydrogen. To make French polish, the shell-lac is simply allowed to stand in the spirit of wine, and occasionally shaken, till it is nearly all dissolved; it is then strained, and is fit for use. The pores of the wood are often first filled with a mixture of plaster of Paris and tallow. The polish is rubbed on with little tufts of cotton-wool until the spirit has passed off, so that nothing remains but a thin sheet of shell-lac. Sometimes gum copal, or other resins, such as SANDARACH, a gum from a kind of juniper growing in North Africa, are added to the shell-lac.

§ 69. **Lacquer** is a kind of French polish used for metals to protect them from the air. It is made of spirit of wine and the lightest-coloured shell-lac, to which is added more or less of the resin called DRAGON'S-BLOOD, produced by certain trees and plants in the East Indies, one of which is the rattan-cane, of which seats of chairs are often made. Metal objects to be lacquered should first be heated, and the lacquer brushed on them while they are hot. If this be not done, the surface of the lacquer becomes dull and grey. Brass door-handles, curtain-rings, brass brackets, and hinges are generally lacquered.

Questions.—What is common varnish made of? What is magnesia? How is it made? What is gum copal? Where is turpentine found? How is oil or spirit of turpentine made from it? How is resin got? What is done to the wood to prevent the varnish sinking into it? What is French polish made of? How is shell-lac formed? How is it cleaned? What is spirit of wine made from? How is it made? What elements is it made of? How is the wood often made ready to take the French polish? How is the French polish used? What is lacquer? How is it used? On what things is it used?

XXVI.

Woollen, Worsted, Carpets, Cocoa-nut Fibre, Looking-glasses.

THINGS TO BE SEEN.—*Sheep's wool—woollen yarn—worsted thread—pieces of carpet of several kinds—cocoa-nut fibre—either a cocoa-nut with its fibre or a drawing of one—a sheet of tin-foil—a small piece of plate-glass—a little mercury.*

§ 70. **Woollen, Worsted.**—The sheep is shorn about once a-year, and the fleece is soon after washed in water. This washes out a soapy substance which exists in large quantities in the wool. It is again washed in soap and water to clean it from grease and dirt. After drying, it is combed between steel combs, which are generally set on wheels and driven by machinery. This straightens the fibres, and separates the longer from the shorter; the former are used for worsted, and the latter for broadcloth. The working of the wool into threads or woollen yarn, and its weaving, is very much like the working of cotton-wool into thread and calico (see § 54). Before combing, however, the wool is rubbed with oil, and the combs used are hot. This makes the fibres slide better, and so lie smoothly side by side. As the combed wool leaves the combing-wheels it is slightly twisted, and then stretched, and finally twisted and spun on spindles, which can be taken out, leaving the worsted as a "hank." The weaving of wool need not be described, it is so like the weaving of calico. BLANKETS are woven loosely.

§ 71. **Carpets** are usually made half of hempen or linen threads and half of worsted. Sometimes the warp is of hemp or jute and the woof of wool, sometimes the reverse. The hemp threads are hard and narrow, the worsted is soft and thick, so that when woven together the worsted hides the hemp. If the projecting loops of the worsted be cut through, the ends stick up, and so give a "pile" to the carpet.

§ 72. **Cocoa-nut fibre.**—The cocoa-nut is the fruit of the cocoa-palm, a tree which grows in most very hot countries near the sea, and which is often fifty or a hundred feet high. It has a straight stem without branches, and leaves only at the top. Close beneath the large leaves, and thus sheltered, hang the cocoa-nuts. These are made up (looking at them from the outside) of a thick husk of fibre matted together, then the nut as we generally get it—that is, a very hard shell—holding the white stuff, which is eaten, and from which cocoa-nut oil is pressed, and, lastly, the water, or milk. The husk is cut from end to end on one side, so as to do as little injury as possible to the fibres, which run mainly in the same direction. The fibres are separated, straightened, and twisted into strings, cords, and cables. The cords are woven into door-mats and matting, which is very tough, and stands a great deal of wear, and is not hurt by wet.

§ 73. **Looking-glasses.**—Flat mirrors, called looking-glasses, are made by covering one side of a sheet of plate-glass (see § 27) with the metal tin (see § 21). This is done as follows:—A very smooth and even table of polished marble is so supported that it can be tilted. Around its edges are rims, and close to the rims are grooves. A thin sheet of tin, called, when so thin, tin-foil, is laid upon the table, and brushed flat with a soft brush. A little mercury is poured upon this, and gently rubbed all over it with a woollen pad. The mercury sinks into and mixes with the upper face of the tin, just as water would sink into and mix with a face of glue. Next, some more mercury is poured on, till the metal is about a tenth of an inch thick. The surface is wiped clean. A clean sheet of paper is laid upon the mercury, wholly covering it, excepting a little space at one edge. The sheet of plate-glass is very carefully cleaned and warmed, and laid upon the table, so that one of its edges rests upon the edge of paper at the end where the mercury is bare. The paper is drawn, and the glass pushed to follow it. The paper wipes off all dirt from the mercury surface and shields it from any falling dust. Dust is almost always flying about. When all the glass is quite above the metal, weights are put upon the glass, and the table is tilted. This squeezes out most of the mercury. Then, after a time, the edges are trimmed with a knife—that is, the metal is cut round close to the glass—and the whole let stand on the slant for a long time, the slant being made time after time greater and greater, till at last the glass stands on its edge. A great deal of the mercury gradually drains from the tin; and a great deal of that which does not drain off passes as a gas into the air. The backs of the mirrors are covered to protect the tin-mercury from rough usage. When you see yourself or anything else in a mirror, what happens is this —The light which comes from the thing strikes the face of the glass; most of it goes through the glass, and meets the back of the glass and the smooth metal at the same time, because they are touching—that is, in the same place. The light is turned back from the metal surface, passes through the glass again, comes out at the front, and, passing through the air, reaches your eye.

Questions.—What is wool? How is the fleece cleaned? What is then done to the wool so as to bring it into the state called "hank"? What is woven along with worsted in making carpets? How is the "pile" of carpets made? What is cocoa-nut fibre? What is the whole cocoa-nut like? What is cocoa-nut fibre used for? Why should it be so used? How are flat looking-glasses made? (divide this question). What is the course of light from a thing which you see in a mirror to your eyes?

XXVII.

German Silver, Britannia Metal, Silver.

THINGS TO BE SEEN.—*Some nickel ore—nickel—zinc—copper—Britannia metal—antimony—sulphide of antimony—charcoal—carbonate of soda—ore of silver—silver—litharge—lime—sulphur—bone ashes—green vitriol—mercury.*

§ 74. **German Silver.**—German silver is a mixture (or alloy) of three metals—NICKEL, zinc, and copper. These are melted together in different proportions, according to the use to which the alloy is to be put. For forks, spoons, tea-pots, and such things, the proportion is about one of nickel, one of zinc, and two of copper. Nickel is found in nature as an ore, which contains arsenic and sulphur along with the nickel. Most of the arsenic can be and is driven off by heat alone, and the rest is driven off when charcoal is heated with the ore. The ore so freed from arsenic is next heated with sulphur and potash, whereupon the nickel and sulphur unite, and can be separated as a solid from the impurities which the potash has made soluble. The sulphide of nickel becomes an oxide by roasting, and the oxide gives metallic nickel when heated with charcoal, because the charcoal joins with the oxygen and goes away as a gas. German silver is used for forks and spoons.

§ 75. **Britannia Metal.**—Britannia metal is a mixture or alloy of tin and a little ANTIMONY, and sometimes a little copper. Antimony is sometimes found as a metal, but more frequently united with sulphur and other bodies. The sulphide of antimony melts very easily; so on simply heating the ore, the sulphide melts first, and collects at the bottom of the melting-pot or furnace. The sulphide, on being heated with charcoal and carbonate of soda (to which oxide of iron is sometimes added), gives up its sulphur, and becomes metallic. Another way is to thrust metallic iron into the melted sulphide of antimony, whereupon the iron and sulphur unite, leaving the antimony as a melted metal. Britannia metal is used for making tea-pots.

§ 76. **Silver.**—Silver is sometimes found as a metal, but chiefly as an ore, containing sulphur, lead, antimony, or arsenic, and mixed with rocks. The ore is broken into small pieces and sorted. Those pieces which are richest in silver are crushed small, and mixed with the oxide of lead, oxide of iron, lime, and charcoal. The lead and the silver both lose their sulphur, and mix as melted metals. The alloy of silver and lead is then put into a furnace and melted, and air blown upon the melted mass, whereupon the lead only is oxidised, and the melted oxide of lead is blown off. At last the nearly pure silver is put in a cup made of bone ashes, and again melted and blown on. The oxide of lead now formed sinks into the bone ash and leaves the silver pure. To get more silver, the pieces of the original ore which were poorest in silver are very finely crushed with water. The whole is allowed to partly dry to a mud. This is mixed with salt and "green vitriol" (sulphate of iron), and mercury is added. The whole is worked together. The silver leaves everything and unites with the mercury. This alloy of mercury and silver, called an amalgam of silver, is washed free from the rocky mud above it. It is then put into canvas bags and pressed. Mercury containing some silver runs through, and is kept for future use. Silver containing some mercury remains in the bags. This is heated in such a way as to drive off the mercury which is collected, and leave the silver behind, and this is freed from any lead in it, as described before. In some places where ores of lead are worked, the lead contains a very small quantity of silver. To get at this without rusting, that is, oxidising all the lead, the whole is melted, and allowed to cool very gradually. The pure lead solidifies first, and can be ladled out by a ladle having small holes in it. The metal which is left gets, of course, richer and richer in silver. At last it is so rich that it pays to oxidise the rest of the lead, as above described, and leave the silver.

Questions.—What is German silver made of? What is it used for? In what state is nickel found in nature? How is nickel ore freed from arsenic? How is the nickel then got as a metal? What is Britannia metal made of? In what state is antimony found in nature? What is the common ore of antimony made of? In what way is antimony got from its ore? In what state is silver usually found? How are the silver and lead of the ore got together free from other things? How is the lead got rid of? How are poor ores treated? How is the mercury got rid of from the silver? How is silver got from lead when there is very little silver in the alloy?

XXVIII.

Plate, Silver-plate, Silvering, Electro-plating.

THINGS TO BE SEEN.—*A clean sheet of copper—a thin sheet of silver—a little mercury—nitric acid—a drawing showing electro-plating.*

§ 77. **Plate, Silver-plate.**—Silver does not easily tarnish or rust. It blackens in the air, if there is sulphur in the air, as is generally the case in rooms where gas is burnt, or into which the gas from burning coal enters. And this is generally the case in towns; for, though the gases from our own fires may all go up the chimney, the gases from other people's chimneys come in at our doors and windows. However, because this sulphur-tarnishing does not corrode the silver deeply, because it is easily rubbed off, because the clean silver is so pretty, and because it has no taste or smell, like iron, copper, and tin, silver spoons and forks, tea-pots, and so on, are pleasant to use, but they are dear. If we coat or cover a thing made of a cheap metal with silver, we have the main advantages of the silver, together with cheapness. To do this there are various plans. Upon a square bar of copper having a clean upper surface, a clean sheet of silver is laid; the two are bound together with iron wire, and into the crack between them a little borax (see § 83) is stuffed in all round. This body easily melts; it shuts out the air, and so prevents the copper from rusting; it, moreover, dissolves any copper rust which may be formed. The two (copper and silver) are put together in a furnace, and by-and-by they stick together and form one piece of metal, in doing which they squeeze out the melted borax and the rust which it has dissolved. The copper bar thus faced with silver can now be rolled, as thin as you please, between rollers, and worked and hammered into any shape wanted.

§ 78. **Silvering.**—Thin coats of silver are given to small pieces of metal by shaking or smearing the articles with amalgam of silver (a mixture of silver and mercury), to which a little dilute aquafortis (see § 127) has been added. The amalgam sticks to the metal, and the mercury being afterwards driven off by heat, the silver alone is left.

§ 79. **Electro-plating with Silver.** — We cannot understand the process at present, but the plan is this:—Some liquid containing dissolved silver is taken; in this are hung, side by side, a piece of silver and the object which has to be electro-plated—that is, covered with silver. In another vessel is put some dilute sulphuric acid (see § 127), and side by side in this vessel are placed, but not touching one another, a piece of zinc and a piece of copper. One end of a metal wire is fastened to the copper in the second vessel and the other end to the silver in the first. One end of a second wire is fastened to the zinc in the second vessel and the other to the article to be plated in the first. Then, on standing for some time, it is found that the piece of silver in the first vessel is eaten away; so is the zinc in the second vessel; but the article in the first vessel is coated with silver. This is called electro-plating, because while it is going on, electricity is passing round and round from the zinc in the second vessel through the sulphuric acid in that vessel to the copper, up the copper, along the wire to the silver in the first vessel, down the silver through the silver solution to the article being plated, up this, along the wire to the zinc, and down the zinc, to where it started.

Questions.—What makes silver nicer to use than cheaper metals? How can plates of copper be coated with plates of silver? How can a thin covering of silver be given to a thing made of another metal by dint of mercury? How is the mercury got rid of? (Do not ask any questions about electro-plating.)

XXIX.

Steel, Tempering, Pewter, Enamel, Borax.

THINGS TO BE SEEN—*Pieces of cast iron, wrought iron, and steel—an air-gas burner, or flame of burning spirits of wine—some water—pewter—tin—lead—antimony—copper—ground flints—borax—soda—powdered glass—an enamelled iron pot.*

§ 80. **Steel.**—Steel is made from cast iron in two ways. In the first, the cast iron is made wrought iron in the way described in § 16, and while hot and soft, passed between two rollers, having each a groove cut round it. In this way the iron is squeezed into the shape of a bar. These bars are cut into lengths, and buried in charcoal in an earthenware pot called a crucible, and the whole is heated red-hot for several days. The carbon of the charcoal gradually soaks into the iron and changes it into steel. The action is stopped before too much carbon has got into the iron. For the difference between wrought iron, steel, and cast iron is chiefly this, that wrought iron contains little or no carbon or silicon, steel contains some carbon and no silicon, and cast iron more carbon and silicon. So that if too much carbon entered the iron, we should go back nearly to cast iron again. Another way is to blow air through the melted cast iron, and so burn off so much carbon and silicon that the metal contains scarcely any, then to add a little iron, which is combined with a large quantity of carbon, so as to make the mixture right.

§ 81. Steel, when heated red-hot and suddenly cooled, becomes exceedingly hard and brittle. The less hot it is when suddenly cooled, the less hard and brittle. So that we may get steel of any hardness in two ways—either by heating cold soft steel to a given temperature and cooling it suddenly, or by hardening it first as hard as possible, then heating it to a given temperature and suddenly cooling it in water. The latter plan is that generally followed; because, when hard steel is heated to different degrees, its surface becomes coloured differently—that is, the colours change with the temperature—so that one amount of hardness is always got on suddenly cooling the metal when it shows a particular colour. This is called TEMPERING the steel.

§ 82. **Pewter.**—Pewter is an alloy or mixture of tin and lead, or tin, a little antimony, and copper. Pewter is used for plates and dishes, and for beer pots.

§ 83. **Enamel.**—Iron pots which are used in cooking are often coated inside with a hard white stuff called enamel. This prevents the iron from rusting, and from being attacked by the juice of the food, which is often acid. The enamel is made of two parts, the white body of the enamel and a transparent glaze. Pots may be enamelled as follows:—The pot having been thoroughly cleaned by weak sulphuric acid (see § 127) and water, and washed and dried, is covered on the inside with a paste made of ground flints and BORAX. Borax is borate of soda—that is, it is the union of the three elements, boron, sodium, and oxygen. Borax is found in China, Ceylon, California, and South America, and looks, when pure, very like washing-soda, and is, indeed, sometimes used instead of that substance for washing clothes. The paste of borax and powdered flint is allowed to dry on the metal. This will form the body of the enamel. To get the glaze, the surface is covered with a powder made of borax, washing-soda (see § 120), and powdered white glass (see § 27); this will form the glaze. The pot with its two coatings is now heated in an oven, so that the flame of the fire cannot actually reach the pot, till the coatings soften.

Questions.—How is steel made from wrought iron? What is the difference between wrought iron, cast iron, and steel? How can steel be made from cast iron without first making the cast iron into wrought iron? How can steel be made very hard and brittle? How can very hard steel be made less hard? How can soft steel be made as hard as you please? What is "tempering"? What is pewter made of? What is it used for? What is the use of enamelling iron pots? What is enamel made of? What is borax? What is glaze made of?

XXX.

Pottery, Crockery, Earthenware, Porcelain, Felspar.

THINGS TO BE SEEN.—*Pipe-clay—Cornish clay—any other kinds of clay—flint—ground flint—drawing of potter's wheel—felspar—different kinds of pottery—crockery—earthenware—porcelain.*

§ 84. **Pottery, Crockery, Earthenware.**—All these are made of much the same things, although they look so different. When pure clay is baked, it shrinks and warps a good deal; this does not much matter for bricks and tiles, but it won't do for cups, saucers, plates, and so on. To make such shrinking less, the clay is mixed with ground flint—that is, silica. The flints are washed, heated red-hot, and thrown into water. This makes them crumbly. They are crushed and sifted, and the powder is ground between hard stones with water. Then it is stirred in water, and the coarser grains allowed to settle. The milky liquid is mixed with clay cleaned in the same way, the water is driven off by heat, and the paste kneaded together. A little "China clay," or "Cornish clay"—that is, granite which has been acted on for a long time by air and water, and so got softened—is added, and the clay is then either pressed into moulds of the shape wanted, or put on a little table which turns round, called a "potter's wheel," and fashioned by the hand as it turns. The shape is made very true by holding up against the turning clay an edge cut into the shape of the outline of the vessel which has to be made.

The pieces of crockery are next gradually dried, and then baked in ovens or kilns like brick-kilns (see § 5).

§ 85. **Porcelain** is not the same as common crockery; because, besides the clay and silica, it has some potash. This is got into it by mixing the clay with FELSPAR, which is one of the things which make granite (see § 11); but sometimes whole rocks are made of nearly pure felspar.

Felspar contains only clay (that is, silica and alumina) and potash. The felspar melts at a lesser hotness than clay, and so binds the other things together, and makes them more transparent—that is, more easily seen through—when cold and hard.

Felspar is used to give a face or hard smooth skin to the finer kind of crockery—that is, to glaze it, just as salt is used to glaze such things as drain-pipes (see § 6). But while salt goes off as a gas, and so touches the things in the kiln which were near it, felspar does not do so, and so, to glaze a thing by felspar, the felspar is powdered and made with water and vinegar (I do not know the use of the vinegar) into a sort of cream, into which the porcelain things are put before baking.

Questions.—What are pottery, crockery, and earthenware made of? How is the shrinking of the clay on baking lessened? How is the flint powdered? What is China or Cornish clay? What is a potter's wheel, and how is it used? What is the difference between porcelain and crockery? What is felspar made of? Why is it used in making porcelain? How is felspar used to glaze crockery?

PART VI.

CLOTHING.

XXXI.

Broad-cloth, Fuller's Earth, Fulling, Teasel, Felt.

THINGS TO BE SEEN.—*Different kinds of broad-cloth—Fuller's earth—fulling teasel—pieces of felt.*

§ 86. **Broad-cloth.**—The shorter fibres of the sheep's wool, such as those which grow under the neck, together with the short fibres which are separated by combing, are used for broad-cloth. These are spun and woven as before described (see § 70). To get rid of the oil with which the wool was oiled, and otherwise to clean it, the web is beaten about under water with a kind of smooth soft clay called FULLER'S EARTH. This is called FULLING. It is then shrunk by being steeped in hot and cold water repeatedly, and is then nailed upon a frame to dry. The next thing is to raise a "nap"—that is, while leaving the body of the web unchanged, to pull out the ends of the fibres without breaking them. This is done by rubbing the cloth with the heads of a kind of thistle called the Fuller's thistle, or TEASEL. The spikes on the head of the teasel carry little hooks. The thistle-heads are fixed in a flat square frame, and the web is brushed with it. Brushes are sometimes used for this purpose, the hairs of which are pieces of steel wire with little hooks at the end. The teasel-frame is moved both across the cloth and lengthways, so as to pull out the ends of the fibres both of the warp and the woof. The cloth so scratched has a nap, but it is very uneven, some hairs being longer than others. It is cut even by being pressed against a very narrow moving knife-blade. This blade is wound like a screw upon a roller, so that when the cloth is held against it, the nap is cut just as the grass is cut by a lawn-mowing machine. Finally, the cloth is folded, and between each fold is a sheet of glazed paper; the whole is then pressed, and the paper taken out; this makes the surface glossy. Broad-cloth is chiefly used for clothes.

§ 87. **Felt.**—Felt is made by tangling fibres together into a kind of mat. Instead of laying and combing the fibres side by side and twisting them into threads (silk, linen, worsted, cotton), and then weaving the threads together so as to make a web, the fibres are torn to pieces and cast into the air, so as to fall anyhow in direction, but so that they make a layer of even thickness. Such a layer is rubbed on a table with coarse woollen cloth until the fibres tangle. To increase the thickness, one can either add more fibres and rub them in, or make a new thin felt and rub it on the top of the first until their fibres lock together.

Felt can be made out of most kinds of hair or wool. It is used for hats. When made of coarse fibres and covered with tar, it makes a good light waterproof covering for roofs. It is more springy than woven webs, so that it is often used for covering floors. The fibres are short, so that unless they are bound together by something sticky, felt is dusty and wears away.

Questions.—How is the oil got out of the woven woollen web? What is Fuller's earth? How is the cloth shrunk? What is the nap of cloth? How is it got? How is it made even? How is the face of cloth made glossy? What is felt, and how is it made? What is felt used for?

XXXII.

Silk, Satin, Velvet, Velveteen, Fustian, Serge, Kerseymere, Merino, Crape, Alpaca, Straw.

THINGS TO BE SEEN.—*A silk cocoon and drawings of silk-worm, chrysalis, and moth—floss-silk—silk thread—woven silk—satin—velvet—velveteen—fustian—serge—kerseymere—crape—alpaca—merino—straw.*

§ 88. **Silk.**—A moth lays eggs which hatch in warm weather, and out of each egg comes a little caterpillar called a silk-worm. This feeds on leaves, and grows, and when it has stopped growing, it presses out of its body, through two little holes in its head, a sticky juice, which hardens quickly in the air. The first of this is stuck by the caterpillar on some solid body, and by moving the head away more is drawn out, and so on. In this way the caterpillar winds around itself an unbroken double thread, making thus a case, in the form of an egg, about as big as a walnut. This is called a cocoon, and is SILK. Then the caterpillar turns into a chrysalis inside the cocoon. The chrysalis is like a large maggot. It has no legs; it has a hard skin. When left to itself in the cocoon, the chrysalis changes into a moth, and the moth forces its way out of the cocoon, lays eggs, and dies. In getting out of the cocoon the moth breaks the fibres. To prevent this, when long fibres are wanted, the cocoon is put into an oven or hot water, or set out in the strong sunshine, which kills the chrysalis. Some cocoons are kept, and the chrysalis is allowed to become a moth, and the moth is allowed to come out and lay eggs. The silk of such cocoons, together with the outside parts of all cocoons, are collected, and form what is called FLOSS-SILK. The inside parts of the cocoons in which the chrysalis has been killed are soaked in warm water, to soften the gummy stuff which sticks the threads together; and the ends being picked up from several, the threads are wound off, twisted together, dried, and wound on large wheels. The floss-silk is served much in the same way as cotton (see § 54).

§ 89. **Satin.**—Satin is silk woven in such a way that the weft thread passes over several neighbouring warp threads, then dives under only one, then passes over several again, and so on; so that most of the weft thread is above the warp. This gives a very smooth upper face to the web; but the two faces are not alike.

§ 90. **Velvet.**—If the loops of the weft of a web woven like satin are cut through, and the ends brushed up and made even, the cloth called velvet is made. To make the web for velvet, flat wires are woven in, and then pulled out, and a knife is passed through where the wires were.

§ 91. **Velveteen.**—Velveteen is cotton woven and cut like velvet.

§ 92. **Fustian.**—Fustian is a rougher kind of velveteen.

§ 93. **Serge** and **Kerseymere.**—Serge and kerseymere are the same as fustian, only made of wool. **Merino** is a kind of sheep's wool.

§ 94. **Crape.**—Crape is made of thin twisted silk threads woven rather open.

§ 95. **Alpaca.**—Alpaca is the hair of a kind of sheep which is wild in Peru. It is woven alone or with cotton.

§ 96. **Straw.**—Straw is the dried stalk of the wheat or other tall grass. The wheat is pulled up by the root before the seeds are ripe, and stacked in mows to dry, and then exposed to the weather and sunshine to partly bleach, that is, whiten it. The bleaching is finished first by exposing the straw to steam, after the roots have been pulled off, and then to the fumes of burning sulphur. It is finally exposed to the air for a time, and is then ready for use. It is too brittle to bear twisting much, but when not too dry it can be plaited. For finer kinds of straw-work the straws are split.

Questions.—How is silk brought forth? What is a cocoon? What happens to the silk-worm after it has made the cocoon? What becomes of the chrysalis? Why is the chrysalis often killed in the cocoon? What becomes of the moth if it gets out of the cocoon? What is floss-silk? How is the silk got from the cocoon? What is satin? What is velvet? What is velveteen? What is fustian? What is serge? kerseymere? crape? alpaca? What is straw? How is straw bleached?

XXXIII.

Leather, Gelatine, Tannin, Tan, Kid-skin, Wash-leather, Chamois (Shamoy), Blacking.

THINGS TO BE SEEN.—*A piece of raw dry hide—slaked lime—glue—glue dissolved in water—oak bark—tan (that is, ground oak bark)—dubbin—soot—tallow—fish-oil—bran—alum—salt—white of egg—pumice-stone—wash-leather—ground bone-charcoal—sperm oil—treacle—vinegar—sulphuric acid—gum-arabic.*

§ 97. **Leather.**—Leather is made from the skins and hides (that is, thick skins) of animals. To make leather from the skins, they have to be cleaned and tanned, and then curried. As skins have often to be carried a long way after they are stripped from the animal, and as wet skins soon rot, they are thoroughly dried, or sometimes salted. Such skins have first to be dressed (that is, the horns, tail, and thin edges cut off), and then thoroughly soaked and kneaded in water to make them soft; then they are stirred about with water containing slaked lime (see § 3). This loosens the hair, which is then scraped off. Next the lime is completely washed out with water, and the skin is put on a wide round beam with the flesh side upwards. Then it is scraped clean from fat and the larger blood-vessels and bits of flesh by a curved scraper; then the skins are turned over and scraped heavily on the other side, to squeeze out as much fat as possible. Skins so treated would get hard when dry. They have next to be TANNED. Skins contain a large quantity of a substance called GELATINE, which is nothing else but glue (see § 25); but in the skin this gelatine is held in little bags, just as the fat of animals is held (see § 41). This gelatine, or glue, becomes quite hard when it is mixed with the liquor in which the barks of some trees (such as oak and willow), or the wood of others, have been steeped. The reason is, that such barks or wood contain a substance called, from its use, TANNIN, and which can be got pure as a white powder, which dissolves in water. This tannin it is which makes the gelatine, and so the skin, hard and less acted on by water. The gelatine is made harder than it is in the wet skin, but not so hard as it is in the dry—not so hard as dry glue. To tan the skins, they are thrown into a pit and stirred now and then for several weeks with water and chips of oak bark. At last they are laid in a pit in a single layer on a layer of ground oak bark called TAN. More skins are spread on this, then more tan, and so on, and the whole is covered with water in which tan has been boiled. Time after time the old tan, called spent tan, is replaced by new, and in about a year the tanning is finished, if the leather is thick like sole-leather—that is, if the skin is a hide. The skins are finally scraped and rolled under a heavy brass roller.

Calf-skins and other thinner skins are tanned in the same way; but before being put in the tan-pit they are kneaded and rubbed for some days with manure.

After tanning, the leather comes into the hands of the CURRIER. The currier damps the leather, and lays it across a board with the side where the hair used to be downwards. He then pares the surface away by means of a knife having a handle at each end, and having the edge of its blade turned round like a hook. By this tool the leather is so shaved that it is equally thick all over. Next the leather is wetted and put on a slate table, the side where the hair was being downwards, and scraped with a blunt edge, and brushed with water with a strong brush. The skin is turned over, and the hair side is brushed and scraped in the same way, to remove a white substance which comes from the tan. When it has been taken from the table and hung till nearly dry, it is painted with dubbin, which is a mixture of soot or lamp-black (carbon) and tallow and fish oil. As the leather dries, the greasy mass, especially its oil, sinks in.

§ 98. **Kid-skin**, as used for gloves, is also prepared for tanning something in the same way, namely, by scraping and liming; the hair is plucked out by tweezers, and the face ground by a flat stone, and the lime is washed out. The skins are then left for some weeks in a mixture of bran and water. The bran ferments (see § 107), and part of the skin ferments, giving off carbonic acid from its pores; this opens them. Next begins the process of tanning. The skins are steeped for a few minutes in a solution of alum and salt. To the alum and salt both flour and the yolks of eggs are added, so as to make a paste. The skins are kneaded in this, and left in it for some hours, taken out, and dried for a week or two. To finish them, they are dipped in water and rubbed with a smooth, hard, nearly flat tool; then dried and stretched, smoothed on one side with pumice-stone (see § 128), and ironed with a hot iron.

§ 99. **Wash-leather, or Chamois (Shamoy).**—Wash-leather, which is used in cleaning glass and silver, is made much in the same way as kid, but from stouter skins, such as those of deer and of sheep. After cleaning and liming, the hair side of the skin is rubbed off with pumice-stone (see § 128). The skins are then steeped in bran-water as above, and washed and partly dried, beaten, and washed often with fish oil. Then they are piled together for a time. The oil is removed by weak lye (see §§ 119, 120), and the skins are washed and dried.

Leather is used for boots and shoes, and gloves and riding-trousers; for covering chairs and sofas; for binding books; for some kinds of aprons; for harness, straps, bags, belts, and many other things.

§ 100. **Blacking.**—Blacking, as used for boots, is generally a mixture of ground bone-charcoal, called bone-black (see §§ 38, 117), with sperm oil (see § 47), treacle (see § 117), vinegar (see § 118), and sulphuric acid (see § 127). In paste-blacking there is less vinegar; sometimes gum-arabic (see § 139) is added. The use of good blacking keeps boots sound, but blacking with too much sulphuric acid rots them.

Questions.—What is leather? How are skins and hides kept from rotting? What is meant by the dressing of the skins? How is the hair got off the skins? How are the skins further cleaned? What is gelatine, and how does it lie in the skins? What is tannin, and where is it found? What is the action of tannin on gelatine? What is tan, and how are skins tanned? How are calf-skins tanned? What does the currier do to the skin? What is dubbin? How are kid-skins handled before tanning? How are they made porous? How are they then tanned? How is wash-leather made? What is leather used for? What is blacking made of?

XXXIV.

Fur, Combs, Ebonite, Pins, Cream of Tartar, Tartaric Acid, Brooms, Brushes, Bast.

THINGS TO BE SEEN.—*Some pieces of fur, with the skin—lard—sawdust—plaster of Paris—pieces of tortoise-shell—boxwood—ebonite—india-rubber—sulphur—pins—brass wire—draw-plate, or drawing of one—cream of tartar—bran—birch twigs—cocoa-nut fibre—broom—bast—horse-hair—bristles—camel-hair, or ermine brushes.*

§ 101. **Fur.**—Skins dressed with their fur on are called furs. Such skins are not tanned. The back of the dry fur-skin is rubbed with salt butter or LARD—that is, pigs' fat—and this is thoroughly worked in. Then the fur-skins are wetted and scraped, just as the skins are treated before tanning. To remove the grease, they are kneaded with sawdust and then with plaster of Paris (see

§ 12). After beating and combing, they are ready for use. Furs are used in cold countries for clothing. Rabbit-fur is used for men's hats. Many kinds are used for trimming women's dresses, for muffs, and the like. Sealskin is the fur of the seal, from which the long, dark hairs have been taken off.

§ 102. **Combs.**—Combs are simply flat pieces of metal, horn, bone, or ivory, or the shell of the tortoise (TORTOISE-SHELL), or boxwood, or EBONITE. Ebonite is INDIA-RUBBER (see § 137) which has been heated strongly with a large quantity of sulphur (see § 49). The sulphur unites with the india-rubber, and forms with it a hard brown mass, which becomes nearly black on polishing. If there be less sulphur, and the heating be not so strong and not so long, the india-rubber forms, with the sulphur, a body known as vulcanised india-rubber, or VULCANITE. This is very elastic, and does not get hard with cold, as india-rubber does, nor does it stick together like that substance. It is used for tubes and elastic bands. The combmakers cut the teeth of the comb by means of two circular saws, as far apart as the teeth of the comb have to be. One of these saws is a little larger than the other, so that when the plate is pressed upon them one cuts deeper than the other. The plate is then shifted so that the larger saw finishes the first slit of the lesser saw, while the lesser one is making a fresh slit, and so on. By this means it is clear that the teeth will be all at the same distance apart; for the big saw in the shallow slit serves as a guide for the little saw to begin its work. Clean cut surfaces of tortoise-shell stick perfectly together, without cement, when warm. In this way large combs can be built up. The rough faces and edges of the slits left by the saw are smoothed by a file and polished with pumice-stone powder (see § 128).

§ 103. **Pins.**—Brass wire (see § 20) is drawn through holes in a steel plate (a DRAW-PLATE), until it has the thickness wanted. It is straightened by being drawn between six or seven smooth iron pegs set upright in a table, nearly in a line, some distance apart, in such a way that the wire passes on one side of one peg and the other side of the other, and so on. Lengths twice as long as the pin has to be are cut off with a chisel, and both ends of such pieces are pointed by being ground, and turned round during the grinding on a steel wheel which turns round, and has an edge like the face of a file. Another steel wheel, with finer cut face, finishes the pointing. The length of wire is now cut into two in the middle. The piece of wire is held near the broad end by some steel jaws having a little smooth hole in them at their very edges, just where they clutch the wire. A little hollow steel cup is forced upon the end of the pin. This squeezes the end of the pin and makes it fill both hollows, and so gives it a solid head. This is a little flattened by a blow with a hammer while still held in the steel jaws. The pins are now plated with tin. This is done by boiling them with pieces of tin and CREAM OF TARTAR. Cream of tartar is tartaric acid united with potash (see § 119). TARTARIC ACID is the acid which is in grapes and other fruits, and which is got in the making of wine. The pins are next dried and polished by being shaken with bran (see § 106).

§ 104. **Brooms and Brushes.**—Brooms for sweeping wet stones are generally made either of twigs of the birch tree, or of cocoa-nut fibre (see § 72), or of the BROOM (a plant growing on heaths, with a yellow flower the shape of a sweet pea-flower), or of the veins of the leaves of some palm trees, or the unseparated fibres of the flax and hemp plants, called BAST. Strips of bast roughly woven together are much used for packing furniture when it is moved. Dry dust is swept from floors and the ground by brooms made of horse-hair. Carpet-brooms are generally of cocoa-nut fibre or bast, hearth-brooms of horse-hair; scrubbing-brushes, boot-brushes, black-lead-brushes (used for rubbing blacklead upon grates to keep them from rust), clothes-brushes, tooth-brushes, hair-brushes, and some painters' brushes are made of hogs' bristles, those of the neck and back being the longest. Dusting-brushes are sometimes of feathers. Some brushes used by painters are made of horse-hair, some of different kinds of fur, the very finest being made from the hair of the camel or the tail of the ermine. Hat-brushes are made of horse-hair.

Questions.—How are furs got ready for use? What are furs used for? Of what stuffs are combs usually made? What is ebonite? How are the teeth of combs cut? How is brass wire got to the right thickness for making pins? How is the wire straightened? Into what lengths is it cut? How are the pins pointed? How are the heads of pins made? How are the pins covered with tin? What is tartaric acid? How are the pins dried and polished? What are brooms and brushes generally made of?

XXXV.

Needles.

THINGS TO BE SEEN.—*Needles—draw-plate, or drawing of one—oil—sand—emery—sawdust—soap—bran—wash-leather.*

§ 105. **Needles.**—Steel wire having been drawn through the draw-plate (see § 103) to the thickness wanted, is cut into pieces a little more than twice as long as the needle is to be. These are straightened by being pressed and rubbed in little troughs. The two ends are pointed and sharpened, without water, on grindstones, which are made of stone, finer and finer stones being used. The doubly-pointed wires are cut in two in the middle by a pair of steel shears. They are then laid flat on a little copper tray, so that their points rest against the raised edge running along one side of the tray, while their thick ends project over the opposite edge. The thick ends are cut off by a pair of steel shears, to which the edge of the tray serves as a guide. The thick ends, where the eye is to be, are laid upon a block of steel, and hit with a little smooth steel hammer. This flattens them. At the same time it hardens them. They have to be softened before the eye can be made. They are therefore heated, and allowed to cool slowly (see § 80). The flattened end is laid upon a block of steel, and a steel punch (a short, pointed, but not sharpened steel rod) is struck with a hammer first on one side of the needle, and then the needle is turned over, and the punch is driven through from the other side. A hard steel wire is now thrust through the eye, and the needle being held with its head on a leaden block, so that the wire is level, a blow is given first on one side, and then on the other. This smooths the hole, and makes it take the shape of the wire in it. Next, grooves, or little gutters, are made, running one on each side of the eye-end of the needle. These are of use to guide the end of the thread in threading the needle. These grooves are made either by a file or by a stamp. The heads of the needle are rounded by the file. The needles are, in this stage, soft. They have to be tempered and annealed (see § 80). Heated red-hot on trays, and thrown into cold water, they become very hard and brittle. They are again heated to a fixed hotness, or till their colour shows that they have the right temper (see § 80). To smooth them and polish them, they are first rubbed amongst one another with oil and sand, or emery (see § 130). The oil and rust is got rid of by shaking them with sawdust. The sawdust is blown away in a sort of winnowing-machine (see § 106). The last of the oil is washed out with soap and water. They are again dried with sawdust, and, finally, are shaken with bran (see § 106), and polished by hand with wash-leather.

Questions.—What are needles made of? How is the steel wire got to the right thickness? How are the needles pointed? What is done to the thick ends before the eyes are made in them? How are the eyes made? How are the grooves over the eye made? How are the needles tempered? How are they smoothed and polished?

PART VII.

FOOD.

XXXVI.

Bread, Sheaves, Chaff, Winnowing, Bran, Bolting, Gluten.

THINGS TO BE SEEN.—*A wheat-plant bearing its ear of seeds—rye, oats, barley, all as seeds—chaff—wheat-grains free from chaff—drawing of flour-mill—whole meal—bran—flour—potash—phosphoric acid—magnesia—lime—silica—iron-rust—sulphuric acid—soda—water—starch—gluten—sugar—gum.*

§ 106. **Bread.**—Most bread eaten in this country is made of wheat. Bread is also made of rye, and oats, and barley. I will describe the making of bread from wheat; the other kinds of bread are made in very much the same way. In about seven months after the wheat begins to grow, it is ripe. After cutting close to the ground, it is collected in SHEAVES (about an armful), and a few of these are piled together with the ears of grain upwards. This is to allow the grain to get thoroughly dry. It may now be stacked—that is, piled together—and kept for a year or two, if kept dry. Or it may be used at once. The wheat is next threshed—that is, beaten with a flail, which is made of two bars of wood jointed together at two of their ends. The wheat is spread upon the threshing-floor, and the ears are banged with the flail, which shakes out the grain from the ear, and also shakes off the husk, or CHAFF. The stalk and empty ear being taken away, the grain and chaff are poured together from some height while air is blown upon them. This blows the chaff on one side, and is called WINNOWING. The reaping or cutting of the standing corn, the threshing, and the winnowing are now often done by steam power.

The wheat is now taken to the mill, and ground between two large, rough, flat, round stones, one being fixed and the other turning upon it. The faces of these stones are cut into a sort of rasp or file; the stone itself is nearly pure silica. The grain, when put into the mill, is covered with a skin; this is so thin and easily bent that it escapes being ground fine, and comes out with the ground grain. It is BRAN; the ground grain is the flour. The mixture of the two, as it comes from the mill, is called whole-meal. What is properly called "brown-bread" is made of whole-meal. For whiter bread the bran is separated by passing the meal through two or three sieves of increasing fineness; the purest flour being that which comes through the last or finest sieve. This sifting is called BOLTING. There is very little difference between bran and flour, as to what they are made of. There is a little more mineral matter in bran than in flour. In a hundred pounds of wheat-flour there are about eleven pounds of water. If a hundred pounds of wheat-flour are thoroughly burnt, there are left about two pounds of ash. In a hundred pounds of such ash there are about thirty pounds of potash (see § 119), fifty pounds of phosphoric acid (see § 50), twelve pounds of magnesia (see § 67), three pounds of lime (see § 3), four pounds of silica (see § 29), half-a-pound of oxide of iron, a quarter of a pound of sulphuric acid, and a quarter of a pound of soda. The proportions of these things vary according to the nature of the wheat and the soil upon which it is grown. The part which is driven off and burnt away, namely, about ninety-eight pounds out of the hundred of flour, is made up of about ten pounds of water, seventy of starch (see § 125), eleven pounds of

GLUTEN (a body made of oxygen, hydrogen, carbon, and nitrogen), and four of gum (see § 139); the remaining five pounds are made of a little fat, sugar, and a body like the white of an egg.

Questions.—What is bread made from? How is the wheat gathered and dried? How is the grain freed from the straw and ear? How is the grain freed from chaff? How is corn ground? What is bran? How is bran got away from the flour? What is whole meal? How much water is there in a hundred pounds of wheat-flour? How many pounds of ash are left when a hundred pounds of wheat-flour are burnt? What is this ash made of? What are the substances which are driven off or burnt when the flour is heated?

XXXVII.

Fermentation, Yeast, Barm, Glucose, Dextrine, Leaven, Ærated Bread, Biscuits, Oatmeal.

THINGS TO BE SEEN.—*Yeast, or a drawing of yeast-plants—starch—gum—sugar—alcohol—bottle of soda-water—potatoes—bread—bicarbonate of soda—hydrochloric acid—biscuits—oatmeal.*

§ 106 *(continued)*.—The next thing to be done, to make the flour into bread, is to make it into dough, and to make the dough spongy—that is, full of hollows. There are three chief ways of doing this.

§ 107. **Fermentation, Yeast, Barm.**—There is a little plant called YEAST, which is so small that you can scarcely see a single plant without a magnifying glass. But when a yeast-plant finds itself in contact with its proper food, it gives rise to other yeast-plants at a very great rate. The proper food of yeast is starch, gum, sugar, and GLUCOSE (a kind of sugar found in grapes and other fruit). As the yeast grows, it changes the starch, gum, and sugar first into DEXTRINE, and then changes the dextrine into carbonic acid (see §§ 3, 8, 31, 32) and alcohol (spirits of wine, see §§ 68, 115). A little yeast will in time change any amount of these substances into carbonic acid and alcohol, and will itself increase in quantity. Such change is called FERMENTATION. To get yeast, some potatoes are boiled, peeled, and mashed with water, flour, and yeast. If kept warm, this soon begins to ferment. It gets filled with yeast-plants. This pasty liquid is sometimes called BARM. Some of this yeast is mixed with more flour and water, and the whole is again allowed to ferment. This is seen by its swelling, owing to the formation of carbonic acid gas within it, which makes hollows in it. Then it is mixed with salt, which flavours it, and checks, but does not stop further fermentation. Lastly, it is mixed with more flour and water, and the whole thoroughly kneaded together. After fermentation has gone on for a couple of hours, the dough is made into the form of loaves, and baked. It is then bread. The heat of the oven kills the yeast, and increases the size of the bubbles of carbonic acid, and drives out the alcohol. Yeast is also the cause of fermentation in making beer (see § 115), and, as more yeast grows in the brewery than the brewer wants, he sells it to the baker, and so the latter may save himself the trouble of making a ferment with potatoes. A small piece of fermented dough, if not kept too long, will start a fresh lot of dough. Such a piece of fermented dough is called LEAVEN. Leaven, however, soon becomes sour, and makes the bread so. Large quantities of yeast are imported in a compressed state from the German breweries.

§ 108. Another way of making bread is to mix the flour with a little bicarbonate of soda (see § 120), and the water with a little hyrochloric acid (see § 120). On making the dough, the acid and the carbonate give rise to water and chloride of sodium (which is nothing else than common salt), and carbonic acid, which blows out the dough. By this means the whole of the flour is kept as bread, and not partly spent in making carbonic acid and alcohol, and there is so far an advantage. Some baking powders contain an acid called tartaric acid. Such baking powders are not wholesome if used often.

The same advantage is got in the so-called ÆRATED

BREAD. If, instead of water to mix with the dough, you were to use soda-water—that is, water into which carbonic acid has been squeezed—and if you could mix the two into a dough inside the soda-water bottle, then, when you took the dough out, the carbonic acid would blow the dough out and make it spongy, just as fermentation did. Machines are made to do this, and the dough merely wants baking to be bread.

§ 109. **Biscuits.**—Plain biscuits (such as ship biscuits) are simply baked unfermented dough. Fancy biscuits are made by adding to the dough such things as starch, sugar, treacle, butter, eggs, and various spices and flavourings.

§ 110. **Oatmeal.**—Oatmeal is generally eaten unfermented, either as oatmeal cake, which is the meal mixed with water or milk, and baked or grilled, or as porridge, which is the meal boiled with water or milk. Most people find that porridge is easy to digest. Some find it more wholesome with milk, others with sugar, others with salt.

Questions.—What is yeast like? What does it live on? What does it change its food into? How is yeast made to grow? What is barm? How is the dough for bread made? How is bread made from such dough? Whence is yeast most commonly got? What is leaven? What other way is there of making the bread full of little hollows of carbonic acid? What is the advantage of this? How is ærated bread made? What are biscuits? What is done to oatmeal before it is eaten?

XXXVIII.

Milk, Cream, Butter, Cheese, Whey.

THINGS TO BE SEEN.—*Fresh milk—milk which has stood a few hours, showing cream—butter—buttermilk—rennet (or hydrochloric acid)—whey—cheese.*

§ 111. **Milk.**—The milk generally used either for drinking by itself, or with water, tea, and coffee, or for making butter and cheese, is the milk of the cow. In some countries the milk of the ewe goat, camel, mare, or reindeer is used. Of course, as young animals feed wholly on milk, the milk they drink must contain every element necessary for their growth except oxygen, which they get from the air. The chief things we need consider in milk is the fat, which gives cream and butter; the substance which curdles, called curds, which gives cheese; and the watery part, or whey, which contains a kind of sugar and mineral bodies.

§ 112. **Cream.**—Fresh milk is a yellowish-white liquid. You cannot see through it, because there are floating in it numbers of very small drops of fat. On standing, these rise to the top, and form a layer which is skimmed off, and is cream; the rest of the milk is skim-milk. Sometimes the milk is heated (but not boiled) to help the cream to rise.

§ 113. **Butter.**—On beating the cream with the hand, or in a kind of tub called a churn, the buttermilk which is still in the cream is squeezed out from between the drops of fat, so that these drops touch and stick to one another. When they do so, they form butter. Instead of letting the cream rise and churning it, the milk itself is often churned, and the butter is so made at once, leaving the buttermilk.

§ 114. **Cheese.**—If you put any acid to unskimmed milk a part of the milk curdles—that is, it turns into a kind of white jelly, called Curds. The rest of the milk is then called Whey. It is almost as clear as water. The curds contain the cream (therefore the butter) and a substance called caseine, or cheese-stuff. You must understand that when the acid is added to the milk, it is this cheese-stuff which becomes solid, and that the cream joins it in becoming solid. If you take this solid, and let the whey drain away from it, you get what is called cream-cheese. If you press the whey out, and let the stuff turn sour (unite with the oxygen of the air) and rot (become a little garden of plants and animals), you get ripe cheese.

Such cheese therefore contains all the cream of the milk. But suppose you first take the cream away, and add the acid to the skim-milk, it will still curdle, but the curds will not contain the fat. You thus get a curd, and so a cheese, which you may call poor, if you call fat rich. Sometimes the fat of one milk (that is, the cream) is put with another lot of milk and then curdled. In this way such cheeses as Stilton and "double" cheeses are made. The caseine, or cheese-stuff, contains a great deal of nitrogen. So do we. And we get all the nitrogen from our food (not directly from the air, although it contains so much—see § 30). Flesh (lean meat) contains a large quantity of nitrogen, true fat none. It comes then, to this, that cheeses made from whole milk, or milk to which cream has been added, are useful to those whose bodies require fat. Those cheeses which have been made from skim-milk are useful to those whose bodies require flesh, always supposing that the same weight is eaten of each kind.

I said above that, in the making of cheese, any acid would cause the milk and skim-milk (not the pure whey) to curdle. Different acids have this power in different degrees. In some countries the acid called hydrochloric acid (see § 120) is used. Cows give most milk soon after having calves, and the stomach of the calf has the power of curdling milk with great ease. The inner skin of a calf's stomach is cleaned, salted, and dried, and is then called RENNET. When wanted for curdling milk, pieces of rennet are soaked in water and added to the warm milk. The whole matter stands thus :—

MILK consists of cream, cheese-stuff (caseine), and whey.

CREAM, beaten, becomes butter.

CHEESE-STUFF, curdled and pressed, and allowed to rot, with or without cream, becomes cheese.

WHEY contains almost all the water of the milk, and also a particular kind of sugar called milk-sugar, and some mineral bodies.

Questions.—From what animals is milk got? How is it that very young animals need nothing for food but milk? How is cream got from milk, and what sort of stuff is it? How is butter made from cream and milk? How are curds got from milk? What is whey? When whole milk is curdled, what becomes of the cream? How can milk be curdled? How is cheese made from curds? What is the difference between cheese made from whole milk and cheese made from skim-milk? What are double cheeses? What is rennet? How is it used? What is cream made of? What is cheese made of? What is whey made of?

XXXIX.

Beer, Sprouting or Germination, Malt, Mashing, Mash, Grains, Wort, Hops.

THINGS TO BE SEEN.—*Barley seed—sprouting-barley (called malt)—dried malt—wort and grains—hops—drawing of yeast plant—alcohol—carbonic acid (as from a bottle of beer or ginger-beer).*

§ 115. **Beer.**—The grain called barley is generally used for making beer—that is, ale, porter, and stout. The ripe grain is soaked in water for a couple of days, then drained and spread in shallow heaps. After a time, the grain begins to grow—that is, to send out a little shoot, which would form the new plant if earth were present (see § 34). During this shooting, sprouting, or "GERMINATION," as it is called, a little of the starch (see § 125) which is in the grain is turned into glucose (see § 107), and the sprouted grain in this state is called MALT. The malt is next heated on a floor called a malt-kiln. This stops the further growth, and gives colour to the malt, and so to the beer which is made from it. The temperature is lowest for pale ales, and highest for stouts and porters. The kiln-dried malt is next sifted on a sieve, which lets the little germ-stalks only pass through.

The malt is next mixed with warm water, and left for a little while—whereupon most of the starch is changed into glucose. The glucose and colour dissolve; the rest of the starch is softened, and little else is left in the seed but gluten (see § 106). The boiling and stirring of the malt with water is called Mashing. The Mash is next drained. The barley which has thus sprouted, and been dried and boiled with water, is called Grains; the part which is drained off, and which contains glucose, starch-matter, and some of the minerals of the grain, is called Wort. The next thing to be done to make the wort into beer is to give it a bitter flavour, and to prevent it turning mouldy. Both of these ends are gained by boiling hops in it. Hops are grown for this purpose. The hop-plant is a trailing or climbing plant, which, when cultivated, is made to grow up poles. The flowers are gathered, dried, and packed in sacks, and sent to the brewers, who boil them with the wort.

Thus flavoured with hops, the wort, if left to itself, begins to Ferment. Placed in a tub, the gas is formed in it, which is called carbonic acid gas, and at the same time alcohol is formed. In fact, this is what takes place:— The wort contains glucose, and this glucose, during fermentation, divides itself into two parts, one of which is carbonic acid, and the other is Alcohol. Alcohol is a union of carbon, oxygen, and hydrogen. (Spirits of wine is alcohol and water.) But when this division is taking place, it is seen that the liquid becomes muddy, and it is found that a sort of scum rises to the top of the worts which are fermenting. This scum is yeast, and this yeast is the same as that used in making bread (see § 107). A little of this yeast put into fresh wort, at the proper temperature, sets it fermenting—that is, sets more of these yeast-plants growing; so that when one quantity of wort has done fermenting, there has been born a very great number of yeast-plants, which can be used in other fermentations (see § 107). Beer, therefore, is a liquid consisting chiefly of water, but containing also alcohol, and carbonic acid, and colouring matter, and some unaltered glucose, with some of the mineral matter of the barley and the bitterness of the hop.

Questions.—From what plant is beer made? How is barley made to sprout? What is sprouted barley called? What is a malt-kiln? What is the difference between ale and porter? How are the germ-stalks got rid of? What happens when the malt is stirred with warm water? What is mash? What are grains? What is wort? What kind of plant is hop? How are hops used for beer, and why are they used? What is fermentation? What gas and what liquid are formed by fermentation? What is alcohol made of? What is the scum which rises to the top of fermenting wort? What is brewers' yeast used for besides making wort ferment? What is beer made of?

XL.

Salt, Table Salt, Sugar, Treacle, Molasses, Vinegar.

THINGS TO BE SEEN.—*Salt—sugar-cane, or drawing of one—beet-root—lime—bone-charcoal—treacle — brown sugar—loaf-sugar—sour beer—vinegar.*

§ 116. **Salt, Table Salt.**—How rain falling on the earth as pure water gradually dissolves and carries down to the sea some of the things which it meets with in its course has been described in § 5. Also in § 8 has been described how carbonate of lime and silica were solidified by animal life, and sent down as shells and skeletons to the bottom of the sea. The sea is made of water and what is dissolved in the water; and to find out what is in the sea besides water, all that we have to do is to let the water pass off into the air, that is, to take some sea water and let it dry. As it becomes nearly dry, little bright grains appear—these are common salt. And so common salt is got from the sea, either by boiling the water away or by allowing the sea-water to dry up. Remember there are many other things in the sea besides common salt; and if you were to dry the sea-water quite dry you would get them all mixed. But it happens that as you dry sea-water, common salt is the first of those things to become solid. In many places, in different countries, the sea has dried up gradually, and the result is that in such places there are great masses of solid salt, called rock-salt, which have got covered with clay and other earth (see § 5). This salt is sometimes so pure that it can be cut out with a pick and sold. More generally it has to be dissolved in water and strained, or allowed to settle, so that clay and other dirt may sink down; it is then boiled, to drive off the water. As the solid salt separates, it is scooped out and put into boxes, in which it drains and dries and hardens.

§ 117. **Sugar.**—The taste called "sweetness" is caused by many different things. Some substances which are entirely mineral are sweet. When a substance which is got from animals or plants is sweet, it is called sugar. So there is a substance found in milk (see § 111) called milk-sugar. Most fruits and many vegetables contain sugar. So do the trunks of trees, such as the maple and birch. The sugar which is most used is the sugar which exists in the sugar-cane and the beet-root. It is called cane-sugar. The sugar-cane grows or can grow in most very warm countries. It is a kind of reed, one or two inches thick, and from eight to fifteen feet high. When it is ripe, it is cut down, and the juice is squeezed out of it by passing it between rollers. The juice is boiled with a little lime (see § 3). Then it can be simply boiled down until it is so thick that, when left to itself, it becomes partly solid. It is then drained. The solid part is brown sugar or moist sugar; the part that drains away is TREACLE or MOLASSES. The brown or moist sugar, when dissolved and filtered through a filter made of bone-charcoal—that is, baked bones—becomes nearly colourless. And this clear solution, when the water is driven off at a low temperature, solidifies as white sugar, loaf-sugar, or sugar-candy. To get the water to come off quickly at a low temperature, the syrup is put into a copper with a tight-fitting cover, and the air is drawn out; on warming the syrup, the water which is with the sugar follows the air, and leaves the solid sugar behind. Thus the sugar is dried without heating too much, and so without browning. Sugar is got from beetroot in much the same way.

§ 118. **Vinegar.**—You remember that when sugar or starch ferments, alcohol is formed, together with the gas carbonic acid. When any liquid containing alcohol and vegetable matter is exposed to the air, the alcohol in it unites with the oxygen, and so becomes sour or acid. And the acid is acetic acid, and the liquid which has thus become acid is vinegar. So one can have wine-vinegar or beer-vinegar. If one wants to make vinegar quickly, the beer or wine is let trickle over shavings, so that it is much spread out to the air, and so becomes quickly oxidised or changed to vinegar. Acetic acid is also got on heating wood in a retort, as coal is heated in gas-making. The acetic acid comes over with the tar, and has to be cleaned.

Questions.—How can salt be got from sea-water? How is it that masses of salt are found in the earth? How is such salt got clean? What substances are called sugars? What sort of plant is the sugar-cane? How is the sweet juice got from it? How is brown or moist sugar got? What is treacle or molasses? How is the brown sugar made into a white syrup, and how is white sugar or loaf-sugar got? How is acetic acid formed? What is vinegar? How is vinegar got from beer and wine? How is acetic acid got from wood?

PART VIII.

CLEANING.

XLI.

Soap, Soda, Carbonate of Soda, Washing-soda, Hydrochloric Acid (Muriatic Acid).

THINGS TO BE SEEN.—*Ashes of wood—potash—slaked lime—tallow and other fats—salt—resin—palm oil—glycerine—linseed oil—rape oil—fish oil—oil of vitriol—chalk—coal—sawdust—carbonate of soda—hydrochloric acid—bicarbonate of soda.*

§ 119. **Soap.**—Soaps are made from oils and fats, both vegetable and animal, by boiling them with potash-lye or soda-lye. Potash-lye is made by boiling the ashes of plants with water and slaked lime; soda-lye by boiling washing-soda (that is, carbonate of soda, see § 120) with water and slaked lime. Soft soap, which is sometimes used for scrubbing floors and for washing woollen cloth, is made with potash-lye; hard soap with soda-lye. To make soft soap, oils and easily melted fats are used; to make hard soap, the less easily melted fats, such as tallow. Let us suppose we want a HARD SOAP. Some washing-soda is dissolved in water in an iron pot; some slaked lime is added, and the whole boiled together and allowed to settle. It is then found that the carbonic acid of the soda has united with the lime, forming whiting, which settles down, and leaves the soda as soda-lye. This is poured off from the whiting and again boiled, and while boiling, tallow is added. After some hours' boiling, the tallow is completely changed, its glycerine (see § 44) being dissolved in the water, and its fat-acids united with the soda as soap. Some of the soap, however, is dissolved in the water; this is separated by dissolving common salt in the water. In the so-formed brine the soap is quite insoluble. Cast into moulds, dried, and cut into pieces, this forms curd-soap. Such soap is rather hard, and does not lather well. To soften it and make it lather, but chiefly to make it cheaper, some resin is put in with the tallow. Cocoa-nut oil is often mixed with the tallow; this makes it softer, but such soap smells nasty, and is half water. A little palm oil improves yellow soap. SOFT SOAP.—The potash-lye, made as above described, is boiled with animal or plant oils, such as linseed, rape, or fish oil. There is this difference between soft soap and hard soap—the soft soap contains the glycerine of the fat, the hard soap does not. If common salt be added to the lye with which soft soap is being made, the soap is changed into soda soap—that is, hard soap.

§ 120. **Soda,** or **Carbonate of Soda,** or **Washing-soda, Borax.**—Carbonate of soda is largely used for washing, both by itself and as one of the things used to make soap of. It is made by pouring oil of vitriol (sulphuric acid, see § 127) on common salt; this gives off a gas called HYDROCHLORIC ACID GAS, and what is left is sulphate of soda. The hydrochloric acid gas is exceedingly soluble in water, and the water solution of it is also called hydrochloric acid, or MURIATIC ACID, or SPIRIT OF SALT. The sulphate of soda is mixed with chalk and coal, and the three are heated together in a furnace in such a way that the flame can play on them. When cool, the mass so got is heated with water, and the clear liquid boiled to boil off the water, while the carbonic acid from burning coal sweeps across it. Then it is boiled to dryness, mixed with coal and sawdust, and again heated. The part of the mass so got which is soluble in water is carbonate of soda, and it is got in the form of crystals by letting the hot solution cool, and by letting the water pass off into the air. Such crystals of carbonate of soda contain a lot of water. If they stand exposed to the air they turn white; this is because the crystals give up water to the air, and at the same time take carbonic acid from the air, and thus they change into the powder called BICARBONATE OF SODA, which is used for making effervescing drinks, because it contains more carbonic acid than the crystals. Bicarbonate of soda is made more quickly from the carbonate by passing carbonic acid gas amongst the carbonate.

CLEANING THE BODY.—The outside of the skin of a human being is always dying, and wants to come away, new skin being formed beneath it. Sweat, which is always coming through the skin, is not pure water, but has in it a lot of salt. So that when the water from the sweat goes into the air, the salt is left behind, and the skin becomes, as it were, pickled unless the salt is got rid of. Oil as well as sweat is always oozing through the skin. Dirt sticks to this oil. To keep the skin in such a state that it does its work rightly, it should be rubbed to get rid of the dead outer skin; it should be washed with water to get rid of the salt. If soap is used, the oil is got rid of more easily, because soap contains plenty of soda to make the skin-oil also into soap and glycerine, which mix with water. So it is good for the sake of health to rub the skin of the whole body with water (to get rid of the sweat-salt), soap (to get rid of the oil), and a rough towel (to get rid of the dead skin). Unless this is done about once or twice a-week, the dead skin and the oil rot, and the skin stinks. And so it is that people who do not often wash themselves all over are so nasty.

Questions.—What is soap made from? How is potash-lye made? How is soda-lye made? What happens to tallow when it is boiled with soda-lye? What becomes of the glycerine of the soap? What is soap made of? How is that part of the soap which is with the glycerine got in the solid state? What is resin used for in soap-making? What is soft soap? How is sulphate of soda got?

How is hydrochloric acid got? How is carbonate of soda got from sulphate of soda? What happens to carbonate of soda when the air acts on it? How is bicarbonate of soda made? What is always happening to the skin? What is sweat made of? How does the salt of the sweat act on the skin? What comes through the skin besides sweat? What is the use of water in washing? What of soap? What of rubbing with towels?

XLII.

Furniture-cleaning, Hearthstone, Flanders Brick, Bath Brick, Sponge, Starch, Prussian Blue.

THINGS TO BE SEEN.—*Oil—vinegar—bees'-wax—turpentine—hearthstone—Bath brick—sponge—flints—starch—British gum (or dextrine)—Prussian blue—iron—carbonate of potash—flour—yellow prussiate of potash.*

§ 121. **Furniture-cleaning.**—Deal tables, dressers, and all wood which is not varnished or French-polished, and which comes into contact with food, are cleaned by simply scrubbing them with hot water and soap. But soap destroys varnish, and French polish, and paint, because part of the soda or potash of the soap (see § 119) unites with the resin of the varnish or French polish, and with the oil of the paint, to make more soap. Spirits of wine also attacks varnishes and French polish. For paint, rain-water and a moderately hard brush, for varnish and French polish, a mixture of oil and vinegar, are the most harmless. Unvarnished oak is usually polished with bees'-wax and turpentine, which does not hide the grain of the wood.

§ 122. **Hearthstone.**—Hearthstone is a chalky sandstone, and is used to whiten other stones, such as door-steps and hearths, by being rubbed over them with water.

§ 123. **Flanders Brick,** or **Bath Brick.**—The stuff out of which these are made is found in the mouths of some rivers as a kind of mud of fine sand, mixed with a very little clay, just enough to bind the grains of sand together. It is used for cleaning knives, fire-irons, and other iron articles.

§ 124. **Sponge.**—This substance is made by animal matter living in the sea, which builds the sponge to live in. It begins to build upon almost any solid body at the bottom of the sea, especially in parts of the Mediterranean, and first forms a kind of stalk, which widens out and becomes cup-shaped as the animal mass grows. The animal matter, which is soft and transparent, is thus protected by its house. The sponges are cut and brought up by divers, then squeezed and allowed to rot in the sand. They are dried and beaten, to shake out most of the sand. Then they are soaked in weak hydrochloric acid (see § 120), washed, and dried. The raw sponge is made chiefly of a horn-like substance; it contains also silica and carbonate of lime. The hydrochloric acid dissolves out the carbonate of lime (which makes the sponge harsh and stiff), and leaves the springy framework, made chiefly of horny stuff and silica. After washing and drying, the sponge is ready for use. Sponges are sometimes bleached, but they are injured and made rotten by bleaching.

The flints which are found in chalk are silica. Most flints are old sponges which have been buried a long time in the chalk which has fallen upon them from the sea above. The original matter of the sponges has for the most part been washed away, its place being taken by silica (see §§ 26, 31).

§ 125. **Starch.**—Cuffs, collars, shirt-fronts, and so on, are generally smoothed, so that dust and dirt may not stick to them so much. This is done by starching them before ironing. The starch used for this is generally made from the potato, but much is made from wheat, rice, or maize flour. The potatoes are thoroughly washed and scrubbed clean, and then rasped, with water, into a pulp. The pulp is stirred with more water, and thrown upon a fine sieve of wire or horse-hair; the water holding the starch passes through the sieve as a milky liquid, while the fibres are kept back. The coarser grains of starch settle first, so that if, after settling some time, the still milky liquid is poured into another pan, the starch which settles in the second pan is finer than in the first. When all the starch has settled down, the clear liquid is poured and drained from the starch, and the starch is allowed to dry. Almost all seeds contain starch, and so do the other parts of some plants. Starch is really made of two things—little skins or bags, and the stuff which is in those bags (compare fat, § 41). If you pour boiling water on starch, it swells and thickens, and when cold forms a kind of jelly; but if you bake dry starch, or boil it for some time with almost any weak acid, you turn it into a kind of gum called British gum, or dextrine, which is very like gum-arabic (see § 139) in its properties, but smells nasty. When linen or calico has been starched, and is then ironed with a hot iron, some of the starch is changed into this gum, and so the fibres and the rest of the starch are all stuck together, the little holes in the web are filled up, and the whole is smoothed by the iron.

§ 126. **Blue, Prussian Blue.**—To correct the yellowness of old linen and calico, the starch which is used to stiffen them is often slightly coloured blue. The blue used is generally PRUSSIAN BLUE. This is a rather complicated body. It is made as follows:—Scraps of old iron are heated red-hot in an iron pot, along with carbonate of potash and animal matter containing nitrogen—any animal matter, indeed, except fat—such as horses' hoofs, skins, &c. The mass, when cold, is boiled with water and strained. Then yellow crystals appear, on cooling. These are what is called yellow prussiate of potash. They contain iron, carbon, potassium, nitrogen, and a little water. The solution of this body, mixed with some solution of iron in acids, gives the very finely divided blue body called Prussian blue. And this blue colour, mixed with white clay, is sold as Prussian blue.

Questions.—How are deal tables and dressers cleaned? How are painted things cleaned? How are varnished and French-polished things cleaned? How is unvarnished oak polished? What is hearthstone, and how and for what is it used? What is Flanders or Bath brick? What is it used for? Where are sponges found? What sort of animal is the sponge animal? How is the sponge cleaned? How is it softened? What is the sponge, as sold in shops, made of? How have flints been made? How is starch made? How is fine starch freed from coarse starch? What happens if you pour boiling water on starch? How is British gum or dextrine made? What happens when starched clothes are ironed? How is yellow prussiate of potash made? How is Prussian blue made?

XLIII.

Oil of Vitriol, Nitric Acid, Pumice-stone, Cleaning Silver and Iron, Emery, Chloride of Lime.

THINGS TO BE SEEN.—*Sulphur—burning sulphur—nitre—nitric acid—drawing of making sulphuric acid—sulphuric acid—pumice-stone—whiting—spirits of wine—rouge—emery—Tripoli-powder—rotten-stone—bleaching-powder.*

§ 127. **Oil of Vitriol, or Sulphuric Acid.**—This, when very much diluted with water, is often used to clean brass plates. It is made by burning sulphur in the air, and then mixing the burnt or oxidised sulphur, which is a gas, with water, vapour, and more air, and another gas made of nitrogen and oxygen. This last-named gas is got from nitric acid (see page 117), and has the power of giving up some of its oxygen to the burnt sulphur, and so burning it further. The gas which has lost oxygen gets it again from the air, and again gives it to more of the burnt sulphur, and so on. The sulphur which is thus thoroughly oxidised or burnt forms, with the water, sulphuric acid. Most of the water can be boiled away, and what is left is oil of vitriol, a dangerous stuff to handle, because it eats away most things it touches.

Nitric Acid, called also **Aqua-fortis**, which is Latin for strong water, is got by pouring oil of vitriol—that is, sulphuric acid—upon nitre—that is, saltpetre (also called nitrate of potash)—or upon nitrate of soda (see § 50). If these things are heated together there is formed sulphate of potash (or soda), while the nitric acid boils away, and can be caught by cooling.

So sulphuric acid is made by using nitric acid, and nitric acid by using sulphuric acid. How can this be? Because a little nitric acid changes a great deal of partly burnt sulphur into fully burnt sulphur, aided by the moist oxygen of the air. In fact we may liken nitric acid, as far as it is concerned in the making of sulphuric acid, to yeast in the fermentation of dough or wort (see §§ 107, 115).

§ 128. **Pumice-stone.**—Pumice-stone is used for rubbing off the surfaces of things, and so for cleaning them. It is a stone full of holes, and therefore light. A lump of it will float in water, but the powder of it sinks, because the grains of the powder are not full of holes. It is thrown out of volcanoes, having been melted; and the holes in it are made by swelling gases, like the hollows in ærated bread (see § 108). Pumice-stone is useful to rub off old paint from wood, and for rubbing stains off the fingers.

§ 129. **Cleaning Silver and Silver Plate.**—Whiting is made into a paste with spirit of wine, and the silver surface is covered with this. When the paste is dry, it is brushed off with a soft brush, and the surface is rubbed with wash-leather. ROUGE—that is, very fine iron-rust—is often used in the same way.

§ 130. **Cleaning Iron and Steel.**—Iron and steel things are cleaned and polished by being rubbed with fine EMERY or ROTTEN-STONE, or TRIPOLI-POWDER, with an oily rag. Rotten-stone is very fine emery, and so is Tripoli-powder. All three are nearly pure alumina (oxide of aluminum); and though a lump of rotten-stone can be easily broken, the little grains of which it is formed are very hard indeed. Lumps of emery are broken by the hammer, and crushed to powder by a beam shod with iron, which rises and falls upon the emery. The powder is sifted through sieves of different degrees of fineness. But for some purposes even the finest sieves would be too coarse, and let grains too large fall through. The finest emery powder got by sifting is stirred up in a vat with water; the larger grains fall first. After waiting some time, the unsettled liquid is run into another vat, some more settles, which is finer than the first; then the liquid is run into a third vat, and part allowed to settle, and so on. The finest emery is found at the bottom of the last vat, and the water above it is clear. Sand-paper and glass-paper are made simply by strewing sand or powdered glass on paper wetted with glue.

§ 131. **Chloride of Lime** (BLEACHING-POWDER).—Chlorine is an element. It is a gas got by warming hydrochloric acid (see § 120) with oxide of manganese—a mineral found in Cornwall and elsewhere. When you let chlorine come amongst slaked lime, the chlorine is absorbed, and the oxygen loosened. Chloride of lime is made by passing chlorine amongst lime. The oxygen, so apt to escape, burns things. Amongst other things which the oxygen burns are the seeds of plants and animals; so that chloride of lime is death to feeble or small living things. Thus it is used to disinfect—that is, to kill living things, such as the fever-germs. I do not think it is yet known whether these germs are animal or vegetable.

Questions.—What is oil of vitriol made of? What is it used for in cleaning? How is nitric acid got? What is got when sulphur burns in the air? How is sulphuric acid (oil of vitriol) made? Where is pumice-stone found? Why do lumps of it float, while, when powdered, it sinks? What is it used for? How is silver or silver plate cleaned? What is rouge? What are iron and steel cleaned with? What are rotten-stone, Tripoli-powder, and emery made of? How is emery powder got of different finenesses? How is chloride of lime used? How does chloride of lime kill fever germs?

PART IX.

WRITING AND PRINTING.

XLIV.

Writing, Pens, Ink, Green Vitriol, Sulphate of Iron, Red Ink, Blue Ink, Oxalic Acid.

THINGS TO BE SEEN.—*Quills and quill pens—steel ribbon—sulphuric acid—gall-nuts—sulphate of iron—Brazil wood—Prussian blue—oxalic acid.*

§ 132. **Writing.**—Paper-making has been described in §§ 57, 58. **Pens** are usually either quills or steel. The quills are generally the longest feathers from the wings of geese. The quill ends of such feathers are thrust for two or three seconds into hot fine sand or into an oven. They are then scraped with a blunt knife, and rubbed with flannel or dry fish-skin. STEEL PENS are made from ribbons of the best steel (see § 80). The ribbons are cleaned with dilute sulphuric acid (see § 127), and rolled between steel rollers till they have the proper thickness. Then, by means of a "punch," a piece is cut out, of the shape which the pen we see would have if it were flattened out, except that the end is square, does not taper to a point, and is not slit. Next, the hole is punched out which you see at the top of the slit. The pieces are next heated, and allowed to cool slowly, whereby they are softened. Next they are bent round, so as to be hollow on one face. At this stage they are hardened, which is done by heating them red-hot in an iron box, so that they shall not rust, and throwing them into oil (see § 80).

After they have been cleaned from the oil, they are tempered by heating them to a certain hotness below redness (see § 81), and letting them cool. Rubbing with sand polishes them. Next the nib is made—that is, the steel is pointed. This is done by grinding on a wheel made of emery powder (see § 130) and clay baked together (in the form of a wheel) into a sort of emery brick. The pen is now laid upon a chisel standing upright, so that the edge of the chisel reaches from the point of the pen to the hole in it. Another such chisel is forced down, and the steel is split from nib to hole. The two chisel edges meet one another in the same way that the two blades of a pair of scissors do. This forms the slit. Next comes the final tempering, and lastly the lacquering (see § 69).

§ 133. **Ink.**—In § 97 you saw how tannin (a stuff which exists in the bark of the oak) is used for tanning skins, and so making leather. There is an insect which makes a little hole in the skin or bark of the leaves and stalks of the growing oak, and lays an egg there. Part of the juice of the leaf which otherwise would form outer wood and inner bark (see § 34) collects and hardens into little balls round the egg, forming a sort of cocoon (see § 88). But the nature of the juice is somewhat changed in hardening, and, instead of containing only tannin, these oak-galls, or GALL-NUTS, as they are called, contain small quantities of a body called gallic acid as well. The nut-galls used for making ink are imported chiefly from Turkey, and the insect which causes them is a kind of wasp. Such galls are broken up and boiled with water. To this, when strained from the insoluble stuff, some dissolved gum is added, and then some dissolved COPPERAS (GREEN VITRIOL, SULPHATE OF IRON). The whole turns nearly black, and this is ink. It turns still blacker when it is exposed to the air, from which it absorbs oxygen, so that ink-writing darkens by time. The gum merely makes the ink smoother, and helps to stick it to the paper. The tannin in the ink also forms a kind of leather with the glue with which the paper has been sized (see §§ 25, 57).

§ 134. **Red Ink** is usually made by boiling the wood of a tree (called Brazil wood), in the form of shavings or sawdust, with water for a long time. The liquid is poured from the insoluble parts, and some gum is added.

§ 135. **Blue Ink.**—Prussian blue (see § 126) dissolves in OXALIC ACID. Oxalic acid, which is a deadly poison, exists in small quantities in sorrel in union with potash, as salts of sorrel. Oxalic acid can be made artificially in many ways. If a mixture of very strong potash and soda lyes (see § 119) is mixed into a sort of paste with sawdust, and heated, oxalate of soda is formed, and this, when dissolved, gives up its oxalic acid to slaked lime, and oxalate of lime is formed, which, being insoluble in water, may be washed clean. This body is, in its turn, mixed with sulphuric acid (see § 127), whereupon sulphate of lime (see § 12) is formed. This gypsum, being insoluble, can be separated by straining, and the liquid which comes through contains the oxalic acid. Most of the water is driven off by heat, and the acid, on cooling, forms crystals containing water. Blue ink is made by dissolving Prussian blue in oxalic acid.

Various inks are made from coal-tar, but they are not very useful for handwriting.

Questions.—What quills are used for pens? What is done to the quills so as to make them ready for pens? How is steel ribbon cleaned and cut into pieces for pens? How is the hole made? How are the pieces now softened? After bending, how are the pieces hardened? How are they tempered? How are they polished? How are they pointed? How is the slit made? How are they finished? How and where are gall-nuts formed? How are gall-nuts used in making ink? What is copperas or green vitriol? What happens when dissolved green vitriol and water in which gall-nuts have been boiled are mixed? What is red ink? Where is oxalic acid found in nature? What is made by heating potash and soda lye with sawdust? What is formed by mixing oxalate of soda with slaked lime? What is formed when oxalate of lime is mixed with sulphuric acid? How is blue ink made?

XLV.

Black-lead, Graphite, India-rubber, Sealing-wax, Gum-arabic, British Gum, Dextrine.

THINGS TO BE SEEN.—*Black lead—india-rubber—shell-lac—rosin—turpentine—vermilion—lamp-black—gum-arabic—dextrine.*

§ 136. **Black-lead**—PLUMBAGO, GRAPHITE.—This substance, when pure, is nothing but the element carbon. It is found in nature, and sometimes in small quantities in a state pure enough to be used for writing. It has then only to be cut by fine saws into square strips, and put into grooves in the flat sides of wooden rods, and covered with other wooden strips glued on the top. Impure plumbago is made pure by grinding it to a fine powder, and dissolving out the impurities with sulphuric and other acids. It is then made ready for pencils by mixing the powder with clay, and baking the two together. Pencils of different degrees of hardness can thus be made; for the higher the temperature and the more the clay, the harder is the pencil. To avoid loss by sawing, the paste of clay and plumbago is pressed into moulds, and then baked. The black lead of most pencils, except those which are wanted very soft, is heated and plunged into tallow or paraffin. This makes it rather harder, but smoother to write with.

§ 137. **India-rubber**—CAOUTCHOUC.—For rubbing out marks on paper made by black-lead pencils, either bread-crumbs or india-rubber is generally used. The two substances act in the same way. Little pieces of the bread or india-rubber are rolled off and pressed upon the black-lead marks. The black-lead sticks to them, and is torn off from the surface of the paper. If you steam the paper on which the plumbago marks are, you soften the size on the surface (see §§ 25, 57), and the plumbago dust sinks into this. When dry again, you cannot rub the marks out in the same way, because the plumbago is now embedded. The writing is "fixed."

Caoutchouc or india-rubber is produced by trees growing in Brazil, East India, Java, West Africa, and other hot countries. Holes are bored in the roots, trunks, and branches of these trees, and tubes or little gutters are put in. A milky juice runs out, and is caught in pots tied at the proper places. A lump of dry clay, shaped like a pear, and having a handle, is dipped into the juice, and then held over a fire. This drives off the water, and leaves the caoutchouc as a skin sticking to the clay. It is again dipped, and dried a great many times. One coat sticks to the other, till the caoutchouc is an inch or two in thickness. Then the clay is broken out, and the caoutchouc is left in the form of bottles, and is called bottle india-rubber. The juice is often simply allowed to dry in cakes. Such india-rubber often contains dirt, and it is not alike all through. It is therefore torn to pieces and worked with water, by being put with water in a round box, in whose inside spikes are fixed, all pointing inwards, but leaning one way, as though they had all been bent by a sweep of the hand. Inside this box is a wheel having spikes pointing outwards, and nearly touching the fixed spikes point to point; the spikes on the wheel are all bent the other way to those on the box. The crude india-rubber being put in with water, the inner wheel is turned round, and the caoutchouc is torn to pieces. It gets hot and soft like dough, so that it is thus thoroughly mixed and washed.

§ 138. **Sealing-wax.**—Sealing-wax is made by melting together rosin (see § 67), shell-lac (see § 68), and a little oil of turpentine (see § 67); the turpentine called Venice turpentine gives the best wax. The red colour of the common sealing-wax is got by mixing with the above some vermilion in powder. Vermilion is a red body got by uniting sulphur (see § 49) with mercury (see § 22). Black wax is made by mixing lamp-black (a fine form of soot, and which is nearly pure carbon—see § 32) with the rosin, shell-lac, and turpentine. The shell-lac by itself is rather too hard to melt. The rosin is cheap, and the mixture of these two melts more easily than the shell-lac alone; but it is too brittle. The turpentine makes the mixture of the two rosins softer and tougher.

§ 139. **Gum-arabic.**—The juice of various kinds of acacia trees which grow in Upper Egypt, West Africa, India, and Arabia oozes out of the tree, and hardens in the air. It is soluble in water, and is used for gumming envelopes.

§ 140. **British Gum,** or **Dextrine.**—British gum, or dextrine, is made from starch, either by heating it by itself in a stove a good deal hotter than boiling water, but not hot enough to scorch it, or by mixing the starch with water and a very little nitric acid (see § 127), and allowing it to dry. After this it is heated as hot as boiling water. Dextrine is cheaper than gum-arabic, but it has a nasty smell.

Questions.—What is pure black-lead? How is black-lead cleaned? How is it made as hard as it is wanted? How is it made into sticks for pencils? How do india-rubber and bread crumbs act in rubbing out black-lead marks on paper? How can pencil marks be fixed on paper? Where do india-rubber trees grow? How is their juice got? How is the juice dried and hardened? How is the india-rubber cleaned? What is sealing-wax made with? How is it made red? What is vermilion? How is black wax made? What is the use of the rosin, and what of the turpentine in sealing-wax? What is gum-arabic? How is British gum or dextrine made?

XLVI.

Printing, Type, Antimony, Printers' Ink.

THINGS TO BE SEEN.—*Specimens of type—lead—antimony—rosin—linseed oil—yellow soap—lamp-black—glue dissolved in treacle and allowed to set.*

§ 141. **Type.**—A left-handed drawing of a letter is scratched by a hard steel point on a soft steel plate thus, . The dotted outline shows the edge of the plate,

The metal is cut away from around the letter, leaving it standing out [Я]. The whole is now hardened (see § 80), and being turned over, is driven by a blow a little way into a thickish sheet of brass. A hole or mould is thus made in the brass, which is right-handed, thus, R. The plate of brass, thus stamped, is made to form the bottom of a little steel box with movable sides. Into this box is poured a melted mixture (alloy) of lead (see §§ 15, 17) and ANTIMONY (see § 75), to which a little tin (see § 21) is sometimes added. An upward jerk sends the metal well down into the mould, and hardens the face of the type. The antimony makes the lead hard; and it has the rare property, which it gives to the alloy, of getting a little bigger as it becomes solid. The alloy thereby forces itself thoroughly into the sharp edges of the mould. When solid, the casting is taken out, its bottom levelled and its sides polished, and it is made, from the face of the letter to the bottom, exactly of a certain length. It is now a type-letter, and is of course left-handed, Я. Any number of types can be cast from the same mould. If the same is done with the other letters of the alphabet, and with the numerals, 0, 1, 2, 3, 4, 5, 6, 7, 8, 9, stops, CAPITALS, *italics*, and so on, we get what is called a fount of type. Types are now almost always cast by the aid of machinery.

To print, the letters are set up side by side in a small frame (called a "stick") held by the compositor, who begins to arrange the type in the left-hand corner of the frame, IИ ꓕHIƧ MVλ. When these letters are inked, turned over, and pressed on paper, the printing appears IN THIS WAY. When the setting of the type is completed, it is wedged up in an iron frame, laid on the press, and prepared for printing.

§ 142. **Printers' Ink.**—Printers' ink is made by dissolving rosin (see § 67) in hot linseed oil (see § 59) which has been boiled until it takes fire when a light is put to it. To this mixture is added lamp-black (see

§ 32), and sometimes yellow soap (see § 119) and Prussian blue (see § 126). The whole is then ground together between iron or hard stone rollers till it gets quite fine and smooth.

The frame (or "forme") of type is inked by rolling its surface with an elastic roller covered with the ink. The roller is generally made of a mixture of strong glue (see § 25) and treacle (see § 117). The liquid glue sets to a very firm jelly, and the treacle prevents the jelly drying up. The paper, which is slightly damped, is pressed upon the type, and becomes thus inked by the type, or printed. These are the chief things about "hand" printing.

Questions.—How is the punch made for making type? How is the type-mould made by means of this punch? What is type-metal made of? What is the use of the antimony? What is a fount of type? How is the type set up by the compositor? What is printers' ink made of, and how is it made? How is the type inked? What is the printer's inking roller made of?

INDEX.

The numbers refer to the paragraphs (marked §).